Praise for Zotti's *Music Therapy*

Art and music play a vital role in people's lives; they offer a sense of reward and fulfillment. Alfredo is a living example of someone living with mental health issues who can be very productive and contribute to the good of the community. With his extensive knowledge and insight of mental illness, he has an empathetic approach and understanding to assist and improve these conditions. Through his own experience of positive outcome by therapeutic use of music, Alfredo Zotti shares the supplemental, holistic method to improving mental health issues and dementia. *Music Therapy: An Introduction with Case Studies for Mental Illness Recovery* promises to assist in the recovery process and help sufferers regain a happier life.

—Rie Matsuura

In my observation, authors with an expertise in a particular field tend to fall into one of two camps: talkers or doers, command HQ or frontline, head office or field. One camp tells you what you should be doing while the other rolls up their sleeves and helps you to achieve it. *Music Therapy: An Introduction with Case Studies for Mental Illness Recovery* was written by a man who is squarely in that second camp. Alfredo Zotti has helped hundreds—perhaps thousands—of people discover the healing benefits of music *from the heart*. At one extreme, there he is at his piano, patiently waiting for someone to learn or rediscover a tune that only they will ever hear. At the other extreme, there he is helping someone to face the world through public performance—and it is Zotti who lugs the heavy PA and stage equipment, supports the performer on stage, invites quality musicians to join the effort, designs the poster and CD covers, spends the hours in the studio and promotes it all through a vast network of music lovers. Alfredo Zotti knows his stuff, obviously, but it's the selfless, hands-on support that creates the magic. Even more astounding, the only reward he seeks is the mental wellbeing of others.

—Paul Wilson, author of *Instant Calm,*
The Little Book of Calm and others

Alfredo's *Music Therapy: An Introduction with Case Studies for Mental Illness Recovery* can be seen as a significant tool in helping vulnerable people. This new book could be used as an insightful companion for music therapy practice. Supporting mental illness recovery by appointing a qualified music therapist is suggested throughout this book. In his humble and generous way, Alfredo shares his very successful approaches incorporating his deep knowledge of music and psychology whereby he continues to support but also embrace people with mental illness. Who doesn't like to read about successful, innovative approaches like Alfredo has worked on? In his book, Alfredo demonstrates that music therapy has earned a rightful place in the journey of recovery from mental disorders.

—Helena Brunner, O.A.M., paralympian swimmer

Alfredo Zotti's book, *Music Therapy: An Introduction with Case Studies for Mental Illness Recovery*, shows that recovery through music can be an extremely powerful and wonderful journey of self-healing and positive discoveries. Music reduces anxiety, promotes well-being, becomes a coping tool and gives sufferers an identity and a purpose to their lives. Alfredo encourages children with autism spectrum disorder to initiate their musical journey through discoveries and curiosity. Because of his sensitivity, intuition and empathy toward sufferers, as well his deep knowledge of music and psychology, Alfredo makes positive changes in people's lives. I highly recommend this book to anyone who wishes to enhance their knowledge of music therapy and the influence of music on their health and, consequently, on their lives.

—Krystyna C. Laycraft, Ph.D, physicist, educator, and artist

Music Therapy

An Introduction with Case Studies for Mental Illness Recovery

Alfredo Zotti

Loving Healing Press

Ann Arbor, MI

Learn more at www.AlfredoZotti.org

ISBN-13 978-1-61599-530-1 paperback
ISBN-13 978-1-61599-531-8 hardcover
ISBN-13 978-1-61599-532-5 eBook

Library of Congress Cataloging-in-Publication Data

Names: Zotti, Alfredo, 1958- author.
Title: Music therapy : an introduction with case studies for mental illness recovery / Alfredo Zotti.
Description: [1st.] | Ann Arbor : Loving Healing Press, 2020. | Includes bibliographical references and index. | Summary: "Provides an overview of some common mental illnesses including bipolar, schizophrenia, Alzheimer's, autism spectrum disorder, anxiety, depression and specific techniques to apply music therapy. Case studies include adults, children, and elders with music making as well as with passive listening. The author is himself a lifelong sufferer of bipolar disorder"-- Provided by publisher.
Identifiers: LCCN 2020036770 (print) | LCCN 2020036771 (ebook) | ISBN 9781615995301 (trade paperback) | ISBN 9781615995318 (hardback) | ISBN 9781615995325 (kindle edition) | ISBN 9781615995325 (epub)
Subjects: LCSH: Music therapy--Case studies. | Mentally ill--Care--Case studies.
Classification: LCC ML3920 .Z67 2020 (print) | LCC ML3920 (ebook) | DDC 615.8/5154--dc23
LC record available at https://lccn.loc.gov/2020036770
LC ebook record available at https://lccn.loc.gov/2020036771

Published by
Loving Healing Press Inc   www.LHPress.com
5145 Pontiac Trail   info@LHPress.com
Ann Arbor MI 48105 USA

Toll free: 888-761-6268 (USA/CAN)
Fax: 734-663-6861

Contents

Foreword by Bob Rich, Ph.D.

Music is the language of God
Ludwig van Beethoven

When I was a terribly depressed young man, I often felt I was an empty space inside a black steel box. Music was one of the tools that enabled me to keep going. I saved some money and bought a small stereo record player and a few records (vinyl in those days). The record player didn't have headphones, but when I felt so far down that I couldn't study—couldn't do anything—I lay on my stomach on the floor, speakers next to my ears. So, I'd lie there, immersing myself in a Chopin piano solo, or Beethoven's "Pathetique" (Piano Sonata No. 8) or the first movement of his 9th symphony (the Choral Symphony) and was lifted out of being miserable me, onto a higher plane of peace.

Running was another of my antidepressants, one I'd relied on since I was 11 years old. Once I found out about music, my 30 mile runs were to the rhythm of something like Dvořák's 8th symphony, from beginning to end. Remember, no headphones or little, portable, electronic devices in those ancient days!

In 1976, Isaac Asimov wrote "Marching In," a short story set in 2001, for *High Fidelity* magazine. Our hero is a trombonist and assists in a mental hospital by playing "When the Saints Go Marching In." All right... sing it to yourself. Does the wonderful rhythm get your toes tapping? Does your breathing free up and follow that rhythm?

Here is a final example of the power of music for good. For the past 10 years (as of the time I am writing this), Australian musicians have made voluntary, pro bono recordings to aid children in hospitals and people in other stressful situations. The soothing tones... well... *soothe*. Calm replaces anxiety. Check it out at www.hush.org.au/hush-music.

In this excellent little book, Alfredo Zotti presents formal evidence for what I know from my own life, and from what I know from observation: music therapy works and is a powerful adjunct to other ways of relieving suffering.

Alfredo has no formal qualifications as a music therapist, or as a psychologist, but he excels in both roles, as well as in many others. He and I have never met, but have been friends and collaborators for over 20 years. He is a talented musician and artist and has written several inspiring books designed to help others.

If he put his many talents to selfish ends, he could be very wealthy. However, like me, he has long learned the lesson that money can cost more than it is worth. Therefore, much of his work is pro bono. All the profits from this book will go to support the Kidman Centre. If everyone was like Alfredo, we would have a survivable future and one worth surviving in.

How can he be so multi-talented? He is an example of the cliché, "If what you have is lemons, make lemonade." He has lived with bipolar disorder for much of his life. His previous books, *Got Bipolar? An Insider's Guide to Managing Life Effectively* (2018) and *Alfredo's Journey: An Artist's Creative Life with Bipolar Disorder* (2014), describe how he changed from a suicidal, homeless young man into a self-reliant, effective agent for social change. I invite you to be inspired by Alfredo, whatever your sources of suffering—turn them into good, for yourself and for others.

Alfredo's challenge is bipolar disorder. He has learned to put his highs to good use, going at triple speed to paint, play and compose music, write and have a positive effect on his local community and beyond. One of his passions is opposing the stigma ignorant people throw at those with (so-called) mental disorders: depression, anxiety, bipolar, schizophrenia, personality disorders, etc.

In this book, Alfredo has not set out to replace music therapists, because each person's situation is unique, and a program of music therapy needs to be specifically designed, to some extent, through trial and error. All the same, here we have essential information that even experienced music therapists will find useful. My evidence for this is that a great many have consulted him.

If you suffer from a "mental disorder," or are caring for someone who is, you shouldn't use this as a self-help book, but will find it invaluable as a guide on what is available, how to apply it, what to expect from music therapy and how to cooperate with a music therapist.

As mentioned previously, during my bouts of depression, Chopin and Beethoven were among my main sources of solace. I used to blast the first movement of Beethoven's 9th symphony, over and over (not the 4th). Very early in my book, *From Depression to Contentment: A Self-Therapy Guide,* I state, "Whatever depression tells you, do the opposite." So, this is the advice to people who avoid music when feeling down. Meditative music, like Buddhist/Hindu chants, Gregorian chants and Hildegard de Bingham can be incredibly uplifting. Aerobic exercise is an instant antidepressant. Combine that with rhythmic music, and what do you get? "Oh when the saints / Come marching in."

* * *

Robert Rich, Ph.D. has retired from five occupations so far, including providing psychotherapy for over a decade. One of his recent books is *From Depression to Contentment: A Self-Therapy Guide.* You will find lots of reading at his blog, *Bobbing Around.* https://bobrich18.wordpress.com

Foreword by Paul Corcoran

Alfredo has written a wonderful book on the topic of music therapy and its benefits for a range of emotional difficulties. As a talented musician and appreciator of music of various genres, Alfredo is very familiar with the therapeutic value of music in managing his own emotional state. As a sufferer of bipolar disorder, Alfredo has found great solace in the creation of music and appreciation for music.

All of us can appreciate the power of music to shift our emotional state. Consider your favourite movie moments and the impact of the musical score in bringing on powerful emotions. Many of these scenes simply would not be the same without the power of music behind them. In addition to the impact of music on our emotions, there is also the profound impact that music can have in re-igniting old memories and connections in the mind. Consider the last time that you heard a song that immediately took you back 10 or 20 years, with all the emotions connected to these experiences. As Alfredo highlights in his insightful book, Music Therapy: An Introduction with Case Studies for Mental Illness Recovery, a systematic intervention with the use of music can be effective in regulating a range of cognitive and emotional processes, producing therapeutic benefits of many kinds.

As a clinical psychologist, I often encourage my clients to have a song or a playlist that they can turn to when dealing with various challenging emotions. I am not a trained music therapist, and the use of music was never a part of my clinical training. However, time and time again in working with clients, I have seen that people will have discovered for themselves the use of music as a self-soothing activity, a means of motivating themselves and a way of improving mood, among many other functions, that music can serve. Music therapy brings a more structured and systematic means of harnessing the value of music in people's emotional health, as Alfredo so effectively captures in this succinct and clear book on the topic.

I congratulate Alfredo on this terrific summary of the ways in which music therapy can serve a complementary role in the treatment of a range of psychological difficulties. Music Therapy: An Introduction with Case Studies for Mental Illness Recovery is a book that can be enjoyed by anyone who is interested in promoting his or her wellbeing or the wellbeing of loved ones.

Paul Corcoran, psychologist

1 | An Introduction to Music Therapy

In this book, I hope to illuminate the topic of music therapy as it is used in a practical, common sense and powerful way to help people who suffer with mental illness and other mental challenges. Unfortunately, governments here in Australia, as in many countries of the world, do not subsidize music therapy in terms of providing mental health insurance for those who cannot afford to pay for it. While this book does not aim to offer therapy that is specifically tailored to a person, it nevertheless offers some elements that can be used by the sufferer to alleviate symptoms. Given that we are all unique, there is always the need for a therapist to guide the sufferer.

Although I am not certified as a music therapist, practitioners of that profession often consult me, because I am a qualified pianist, composer and sound engineer and have recorded many CDs for a variety of artists. Since 1993, as a composer, I have been a member of the Australian Performing Rights Association (APRA) and the Australian Mechanical Copyright Owners Society Limited (AMCO). Recently, I completed my own jazz CD to raise funds for the Kidman Centre. It is particularly relevant that my wife and I also suffer with bipolar disorder, and I have collaborated with psychologists and psychiatrists on various issues. I have also written three books, including this one, on mental illness, and one on art therapy in collaboration with other writers. I have a university degree at honors level, majoring in sociology, anthropology and three years of psychology.

In the following chapters, we will discuss practical ways in which I have been able to help people, of all ages, with Alzheimer's, autism, anxiety, depression, bipolar disorder and schizophrenia. Music therapy can be powerful, either in combination with medical interventions or as a sole therapy, where medical interventions fail, because not all people respond to medication. Over the years, I have developed my own unique methods of helping people and this has also been possible because of my tertiary studies in sociology, anthropology and psychology. When possible, the chapters are supported by research, and I indicate issues in which there is need of more research.

What is Music Therapy?

Music therapy is defined by Bruscia (2014, p.12) as:

> A systematic process of interventions wherein the therapist helps the client to promote health, using musical experiences, and the relationships that develop through them, as dynamic forces of change.

Alvin (1966, p 11) offers a somewhat deeper definition, although complementary to Bruscia's:

> Music therapy is the controlled use of music in the treatment, rehabilitation, education and training of adults and children suffering from physical, mental and emotional disorder. Since it is a function of music in which music is not an end in itself, its therapeutic value is not necessarily related to the kind of music used, nor to the standard of musical achievement. Its effect is primarily due to the influence of sound on man, of which music was born, and whose curative, harmful or negative value will become apparent... throughout history.

Koelsch (2009) proposed that five factors contribute to the effects of music therapy: modulation of attention, modulation of emotions, modulation of cognition, modulation of behaviors and modulation of communication. Koelsh (2009, pp. 26-27) writes:

> These processes can have beneficial effects on psychological and physiological health. Music can evoke strong emotions and reliably affect mood... Music-evoked emotions can modulate activity in all limbic and paralimbic brain structures.

I will now, in turn, discuss each of these effects of music.

Attention Modulation

This is a complicated area of the music therapy. For example, according to Koelsch, when music captures our attention, we can become distracted from any stimulus that can lead to negative thoughts or experiences. For example, suppose a person is constantly worried about personal problems; for example, finances. A song or a nice tune comes on the radio, and the person begins to focus on the music and temporarily puts aside his/her financial problems. However, it is not always this simple. For example, some depressed or anxious people do not like listening to any music at all. They may be completely locked in their negativity and not want to listen to any music, unless they force themselves to do so and then let the therapeutic process begin.

For people with a mental disorder, there must be an initial struggle for music therapy to work. Songs, or some music, can worsen the worries, rumination, anxiety or depression. When one engages in any therapy process, one has to struggle and this is so for any person with mental illness. The struggle is the decision to accept that the person will give therapy a go, that they will attempt to work with the therapist and that they are ready to change. Change always comes at a cost—it is not something that happens naturally. In mental illness, changing is extremely difficult because one must admit that one has problems and that one will work with the therapist to attempt to solve the problems or at least reach a plateau where the problems are less disruptive in their life.

Modulation of attention is an important factor in music therapy, but a therapist must know how to use it and the sufferer must be prepared to do some work. A therapist cannot do the work for the patient.

To recap, modulation of attention happens when the person in question begins to attentively listen to the right music, which helps to distract from negative thoughts that may lead to negative experiences. The right songs or music is subjective, and therefore it is up to each person to find the kind of music that is helpful, either alone or with the aid of a music therapist.

Emotion Modulation

According to Koelsch (2009), some studies have shown that music can be used to regulate certain activities in the brain, which have to do with modulation, generation, termination, initiation and maintenance of emotions. For example, think of a person who has lost a loved one but is unable to cry. Simply listening to an appropriate song, let's say for example, "Danny Boy" (Frederic

Weatherly, 1913), can trigger tears, therefore opening that tap of emotions that need to be released. Many studies clearly show that there are enormous benefits in crying, particularly for people in distress (Becht, & Vingerhoets 2002; Cornelius 1997).

Koelsch and Jancke (2015) write that recent findings suggest that music evokes effects on the activity of the heart, as reflected in electrocardiogram amplitude patterns. This indicates that, when listening to music that has a calming effect, patients with heart disease show a reduction of pain and anxiety associated with a lower heart rate and lower blood pressure. Additionally, heart rate (HR) and respiratory rate (RR) are higher in response to exciting music compared with tranquilizing music. Koelsch and Jancke (2015) call for more research into the effects of music on wellbeing and health, particularly for heart and respiratory related problems.

Music can affect physiological changes regarding heart activity, blood pressure and breathing. For example, because anxiety is a disorder that has largely to do with breathing, some music can be particularly efficient in relieving anxiety and regulating breathing (ibid). Tranquil music, as opposed to exciting music, can control heart rhythm, particularly if at 60 beats per second, which is roughly the rate of a normal heart. A tune that has a 60 beats per second, coupled with beautiful harmonies and interesting melodies, appeal to many people and can be used to relieve anxiety.

Cognition Modulation

Music modulates thinking (Koelsch, 2009; Khalfa, et al., 2008; Nilsson 2009); for example, memory processes, such as the encoding and decoding of musical information. This is particularly notable in Alzheimer's disorder and dementia, where music and songs can stimulate memories (Blackburn & Bradshaw 2014; Johnson & Chow 2015). Modulation of cognition has also to do with syntax and musical meaning.

Behavior Modulation

Modulation of behavior, according to Koelsch (2009), happens when music affects behavior, such as a runner who wears headphones and runs in synchrony to the beat of the music, or a dancer who dances to the music. Music can aid in rehabilitation of body movements and can also modulate speaking behavior. We can breathe to the music, as is the case when we do guided relaxation with music. More radical changes are noted in autism, where children, if helped early, can dramatically change their behavior with the aid of music. One obvious change is socializing through music activity, which then progresses to personal socialization. Coordination of movements, such as the ability to control one's distorted thinking or emotions, as in bipolar disorder, are all dramatic changes induced by music.

Communication Modulation

Music is a means of communication, and language and music often work together. Music improvisation is a non-verbal language, but can also be a pre-verbal language, as suggested by Geretsegger et al., (2004). Classical musicians can communicate emotions without words and sometimes musical expression can go much further than words to express certain feelings; for example, when jazz musicians play together and improvise. In addition, communication through music alone can happen at a much more emotional level, allowing a struggling person to better process their personal struggles. We all know the power of music in expressing love. Or think of how a film scene is enhanced by the score and how the music makes what is communicated to the viewer so much more powerful. Animals also use sounds to communicate emotions, feelings and needs.

There is little research to better understand music as a language and a means to communicate what the spoken word may gloss over. When I choose the right musicians for one of my recordings, I always ensure that I can communicate musically with them. Music phrases and drum fills or improvisations really depend on the quality of musical communication that happens among the musicians and how well they synchronize their performance. This is not like a verbal language, but it is a communication that relies on expression of emotions, timing and skills of the musicians in presenting and performing musical phrases and rhythms. When I sit at the piano, I can communicate my emotional and sometimes intellectual state of mind: I can communicate a mental state of calmness and reflection or confusion and upset.

Music is, above all, a universal language, but it is unique in that it does not have a fixed meaning. The same song, in the same society, in different contexts, can have very different meanings. As Blacking (1995, p. 237) argues, "Not only can the 'same' patterns of sound have different meanings in different societies, they can also have different meaning within the same society because of different social contexts." Music gives us comfort when we have problems. Also, when a society has problems, music is affected. I would argue with Blacking that even verbal language can have similar problems; for example, when we write to another person online and are, therefore, unable to see the recipient's facial expressions. Talking face-to-face helps in defining meaning, and, without it, we can misinterpret the intention of the communicator. Expressing ideas digitally, using symbols and words alone, has its problems, and the meaning of the words can be misinterpreted, or interpreted in various ways.

Looking back at history, we can note how the Charleston Dance suddenly died out at the end of the 1920s, and, by 1930s, it was gone. Some factors affected this, including the arrival of the Great Depression. And we also note the increased output of creativity after World War II, with music suddenly flourishing (e.g., Glen Miller's big band music; Gershwin). We also note that from the tension of the1960s during the Vietnam War, a new musical expression marked the beginning of a special era in pop, country, jazz rock and blues music. Indeed, the 1960s were a great time for music. Today again, I suspect, we are going to have music help us to alleviate all the tension generated by many problems that give rise to great uncertainty.

Due to climate change, pandemics, economic collapses and more generally a world in trouble, we will rely on music a lot more. Particularly, the younger generation will rely on music to cope with a difficult world, and I predict a new era in music as a new critical consciousness emerges due to suffering and uncertainty. Music is, after all, part of the way humans communicate. While some research has attempted to shed light on the communicative powers of music, more is urgently needed, because music as communication is a very complex enquiry. For example, Cross and Woodruff (2009, p. 23) propose that:

> Music is a communicative medium with features that are optimized for the management of situations of social uncertainty, and that music and language constitute complementary components of the human communicative toolkit. It presents a theory of meaning in music, and compares its implications with those of a recent theory of prosodic features of language.

Prosodic is an important word that is seldom used but which has an important meaning in music therapy. According to Vocabulary.com:

> *Prosody* is the rhythm and sounds used in poetry. Kids who can freestyle rap fit the prosody of their words to a rhythm that's already laid down. Prosody can also mean the study of the rhythms and sounds of language, and sometimes you can talk about the prosody of prose. It's about where the emphasis falls in the words and how those work together. When you read great writers like Alice Munro aloud, you will see that their prosody, as much as anything, is what carries the story forward.

That music is a universal language was an idea supported by Charles Darwin (1872), who suggested that "music captures the relationship between affective state and sound that are found across a wide range of species, embodying in the musical signal clues as to the emotional state of its producer." (Cross and Woodruff, 2009) Darwin also noted that, "This leaves unexplained the more subtle and more specific effects that we might call the musical expression of the song."(1872, p.34) It also means, and I agree with Darwin, that we are ignorant of just how powerful music is because of lack of knowledge. When it comes to mental illness, which is a very mixed bag, we should always use as many interventions as possible toward better health, and music therapy is certainly powerful.

There are two fundamental kinds of approaches in music therapy, namely the receptive method (based on listening to music) and the active method (based on playing an instrument). In this book, we will deal mainly with the receptive method.

Problems that Music Therapists Face

Because music is so personal, we likely forget that not everyone likes music and that only a handful of people like every type of music. The reality is that most people prefer certain genres, songs or artists. When they come across a song that they dislike, some people can become anxious. It is of the utmost importance to remember that music therapists use music as a complementary tool to the therapy that they are providing, and that it doesn't matter what music works as long as the patient likes it and as long as it is of benefit to the patient, even if this is to be loud heavy metal music that makes the therapist uncomfortable. Unfortunately, the therapist, in this circumstance, must struggle to show agreement with the sufferer if it is of benefit to the sufferer.

Another problem that music therapists often come across is that music is not a cure for everything, and there are times when it simply does not work for some people. We have to accept this fact; indeed, there are rare cases where music can create problems if used incorrectly or if a particular person is non-responsive. It is important for new therapists to realize that there are times where they will fail because music is not indicated in all circumstances. However, it is comforting and reassuring to know that music is a wonderful therapeutic tool that can help many people achieve better health, and while we cannot help everyone, we can certainly help a great number of the people.

Training of music therapists is quite difficult and it requires that the student has training in music (and he/she needs to play an instrument well) before he/she commences the degree. The degree includes at least four years of intense study, which incorporates 1200 hours of practical training.

The music therapist should be a good performer and be able to improvise on an instrument of choice. The good music therapist should have knowledge of how to arrange a big orchestra, how to conduct, how to teach music, be fluent in most genres of music and have the basic psychological knowledge that relies on evidence-based practices. However, none of this extensive knowledge is valuable without the right personality. The music therapist needs to be a healer-musician and be able to create interpersonal relationships with the patient, which is the main thing that affects therapy. Following the theories of Rogers (1951) and his humanistic psychology, we come to understand today that the "humanistic approach" or "client centered approach" is necessary for an appropriate understanding of personality, without which it is impossible to truly help sufferers. The music therapist should have a stable, mature personality, the ability to communicate well, to share and observe, to show warm sympathy and understanding without becoming emotionally involved, to have a sense of humor and to be patient and tolerant—whatever happens (Alvin, 1966: p. 162).

Having said this, let us now go deep into the world of music therapy by exploring some important issues.

2 | How Can Music Help People with Alzheimer's?

Today, particularly in first world countries, we face unprecedented population aging due to a decrease in fertility rates and growth in life expectancy. Improved technologies, better hygiene and better health all contribute to an ageing population. It is projected that the proportion of people over 60 will increase from 10% in 2000 to 21.8% in the year 2050 (Lutz et al., 2008). There is growing research interest in two fields: identifying aging and prevention of neurodegenerative diseases, such as Alzheimer's (Alzheimer's disease is one form of dementia that can only be diagnosed after death by examining certain brain structures). Because of the population surge of seniors, neurodegenerative diseases and other health problems characteristic of older people will increase (Bishop et al., 2010).

Research suggests that listening to songs, singing or playing an instrument can provide emotional and behavioral benefits for people with Alzheimer's disease and other types of dementia (Balbag et al. 2014). Research on twins has shown that playing a musical instrument from an early age can help in the prevention of neurodegenerative disease, such as dementia (Balbag et al. 2014)

Musical memories are often preserved in conditions that affect memory, because key brain areas that are linked to musical memories are relatively undamaged by the diseases. (Balbag et al. 2014). Why music memories are unaffected in dementia is not understood yet, and we need further research to better understand what is happening.

It is now common knowledge, and I could give many references here, that music can relieve stress, lower heart-rate and reduce anxiety and agitation. Music can also benefit caregivers by reducing their anxiety levels, promoting positive mood and providing a way to connect with loved ones who have dementia, particularly those with difficulties in communicating.

Research indicates that individuals with cognitive decline, which often develops into Alzheimer's, benefit from music listening programs that enhance subjective memory functions and also objective cognitive performance (Nicholas et al., 2010, 2012). Many of the memories of the past may be lost, but listening to music can help improve short and long term memory for the present and the future.

Music taps into brain networks that are still relatively functional. Science is beginning to show how music helps people with dementia. fMRI scans have revealed that music stimulates not only the activity of individual brain networks, but also communication among said networks. Areas stimulated are the salience network, the executive network and the cerebellar and corticocerebellar networks. (Groussard et al., 2010). Not long ago, I watched a YouTube film about Henry, a dementia sufferer who was depressed and confined to his chair, but after listening to music of his era, changed dramatically. "Man in Nursing Home Reacts to Hearing Music from His Era" and other resources mentioned in this book are available on www.AlfredoZotti.org/music-therapy.

In dementia, the language and the visual memory pathways are damaged, and as the disease progresses, things can deteriorate further. However, the fact remains that personalized music programs can activate parts of the brain that are still functional, because musical memories are relatively undamaged. Music memory is independent of other memory systems (Eustache et al., 1990; McChesney-Artkins et al., 2003; Samson and Peretz, 2005., Finke et al., 2012). I will discuss later in the book that the brain is plastic, and some areas of the brain can take over operations that were once carried out by damaged parts. Brain networks can alter to assign various tasks to new areas to make up for the damage. We know that this is possible—not in all cases, of course—but in many instances.

Whether music memories, which are relatively unaffected by dementia, can take over normal memory functions remains the question that no research is directly addressing, although some have touched upon this idea. For example, Groussard et al. (2010) note that musical expertise critically modifies long-term memory processes and induces structural and functional plasticity in the hippocampus. When I was helping caregivers of and sufferers from dementia, I noticed some evidence to support the hypothesis that music memory areas of the brain could take over normal memory functions.

My particular interest in assisting caregivers and sufferers as a volunteer online helper is to find out if there is any way in which music memory areas of the brain can aid in the improvement of damaged normal memory areas. The idea came to me after reading Dr Doidge's book, *The Brain the Changes Itself* (2010). Given the evidence from research, I thought of an additional idea to be tested: to find out to what extent music—specifically, starting to play a musical instrument (particularly the piano)—could aid in this process.

Case study: George and Sandy's Story

One day, I looked at my report on George, an 89 year old man with Alzheimer's, who had a caregiver, Sandy. When I first began to talk to Sandy, she was suffering with depression, and we were communicating on *Depression Connect*, an American website of Health Central. In the first message, she told me all about how looking after her grandfather, who was living with her, was taxing on her mental health. The simple fact that he was withdrawn from life, depressed and confined to his armchair was enough to make Sandy feel depressed.

I thought long and hard, and because I am a musician, and am very aware of how wonderful music can be in lifting moods, I suggested to Sandy that she purchase a secondhand Macintosh computer. There is no need for the latest model for the purpose of creating a musical juke box—any old working computer will do. So, for about $40, she got an old iMac G3, one of those all-in-one computers that were so popular in the late 1990s. I told her how to clean it and delete all unnecessary files. We then proceeded to select music that George liked. Although this was a long and painstaking process, Sandy finally had a collection of nearly one hundred songs, and, as she told me, she knew what songs to use in different circumstances to help George.

George's favorite artists were Al Martino, Tony Bennett, Frank Sinatra, Ella Fitzgerald, Louis Armstrong and George Gershwin. Sandy loaded all of the songs into iTunes and now had a music library which she expanded as time went on. She immediately saw tremendous improvements in George. He now walked occasionally, even sang along and danced, and this lifted Sandy's mood, too. As Sandy told me, George's blood pressure was almost normal now, his pulse was regular and he seldom became anxious. Generally speaking, according to the doctor, his health improved. However,

George still had problems with his memory; for example, he often forgot who I was, while communicating at the computer with Sandy. Sometimes, he mentioned the name Alfredo, after Sandy had told him all about me, and then after a day all would be forgotten. Mood and quality of life had improved, but not so much the memory, which was still a problem.

A great idea came to me one night: I wanted to see if learning to play the piano could further help George. This was a wild idea in that playing the piano is not something easy and not to be taken casually. It was a difficult thing to begin to learn the piano at George's age, but given that Sandy told me that she had an electric piano at home, and that she'd once played the piano in a band, I thought it was worth a shot. I asked Sandy what she thought of the idea and she agreed immediately. She was also curious: "Let's try it," she said, and so we did.

The following week we began to teach George the piano, I remotely via computer and Sandy directly. She had a Roland piano, which is pretty good, with the real heavy action of a grand piano. We began with the book by C. L. Hanon, *The Virtuoso Pianist in Sixty Exercises for the Piano* (1928); I have my own copy I use for regular exercise. Given that George had a damaged memory, we began with just three short exercises, and although they were played repetitively, George loved playing these even for long periods of time. Soon, more exercises were added, and now George was beginning to remember a couple of exercises here and there, as well as beginning to read music and play easy pieces. After about a year and a half of doing exercises and listening to his favorite music, George began to remember my name, and he even began to speak to me. As Sandy told me, there was no question that George's memory had improved. He could now remember basic things. His memories of the past had been severely affected but memories of the present and future had improved. For me, this was a sign that music memories can, indeed, take over the function of normal memory areas and for this we desperately need research.

I have kept in touch with George over the years, and we have not only discussed music, but also put together little songs with the specific purpose of aiding George's memory. For example, we wrote a song to help George remember a particular task, name, date or whatever was important for him to remember. Our online conversations over Skype or Facebook happened on Wednesday mornings, so we wrote a little song to remind George that on every Wednesday at 10 am, he had an appointment with me. This worked like a charm and helped George become independent in his decision to contact me at that time and speak to me. For someone with Alzheimer's, this was a watershed and a welcome relief. No doubt it boosted George's confidence and restored his trust in himself. No longer was he a slave to his disease. He was now able to do basic things and to remember certain things. George's memory has been improving gradually over time—it is not perfect, and George relies on songs to do and remember many things. But, at the very least, this works for him and gives him the power to function reasonably normally, despite his disability.

My personal research tends to indicate that, in the case of a person like George, with dementia, music memories do help normal memories if combined and used together to do important things. It is not easy to achieve this, and it takes courage, dedication, extremely hard work and patience. But there is a light at the end of the tunnel, and this is why music therapy, much neglected by governments and health professionals, is a powerful tool in the management and improvement of Alzheimer's/dementia disease symptoms.

To conclude, I can confidently say that while music helps people with advanced dementia in limited ways, the real benefit is for those people who learned to play a musical instrument at an early age. Preventative measures are always the preferred method. It makes sense, therefore, to say that our world needs to give more importance to music. As the world population ages, it makes perfect sense to make music, and playing an instrument should be compulsory in schools. Music should be just as important as science, because a science deprived of art is incomplete. School children should be encouraged to pick up an instrument and learn to play from an early age and continue to play throughout life. Undoubtedly, this would not only be a good preventative measure against dementia, but also lead us to a more advanced world. Music helps humanity to develop.

3 | Defining Mental Illness

Before discussing how music therapy can assist people with mental illness, it is important to have a look at what we mean when we use the term. There are a variety of ways to look at this concept. My particular perspective is based on the ideas that I share with my longtime friend Bob Rich, PhD. Together, we have devised a theory for which there is lots of evidence, including the Adverse Childhood Experiences (ACE), undertaken in America in the mid 1990s. It is one of the largest longitudinal studies ever. According to this research, the majority of mental disorders can be traced back to a childhood traumatic experience, such as sexual, physical or verbal abuse. The ACE study, which is the largest investigation ever conducted to determine the link between childhood maltreatment and later life development of a mental disorder, shows a strong association between childhood traumatic experiences and adulthood high-risk health behaviors, such as smoking, alcohol and drug abuse, promiscuity, severe obesity and is correlated with ill health, including depression, heart disease, cancer, chronic lung disease and shortened lifespan.

The trauma can lead to serious mental illness such as psychosis and schizophrenia, but more specifically hallucinations, such as voices commenting and command hallucinations (Read et al., 2005). For these reasons, the same authors ask researchers and therapists to routinely ask clients about childhood trauma when trying to understand or assist people diagnosed with psychosis or schizophrenia (ibid). More importantly, they argue that an understanding of how childhood trauma leads to psychosis or schizophrenia requires the integration of biological, psychological and social paradigms that acknowledge the fact that traumatic experiences, particularly during delicate and formative years, such as childhood, can easily alter brain functions (ibid).

According to Maté (2010), an addiction is almost always a way to cope with past trauma and this can be addiction to plastic surgery, to self- harm, to alcohol, to drugs, to spending and buying excessively (to the point of going bankrupt) and to almost anything that is considered to be a problem and unhealthy. (ibid). For Maté, there is no doubt that the majority of mental disorders are due to childhood traumatic experiences.

In 2012, I consulted over 200 therapists from all over the world concerning the causes of mental illness. They included psychologists and psychiatrists, such as Bob Rich, Paul Corcoran, David Butler and many others. I emphasized that I wanted to know about events in a person's history, rather than biological mechanisms. The answer was pretty much the same: it is mostly trauma that causes mental illness.

Childhood traumatic experiences, such as sexual abuse, verbal abuse, physical abuse and being bullied, cause approximately, going by my statistical analysis of what these therapists told me, 70 to 80% of all mental illness in the world. That is huge! I was shocked, but then I had to go and consult my notes from the many people with mental illness I had been helping for some years. There it was—most of the people I had been helping had developed a mental illness due to severe traumatic experiences.

The rest of mental illnesses, according to my notes and what the many therapists around the world had told me, were due to adult trauma (for example, witnessing a horrific car accident where people were seriously hurt) and sexual abuse in women. Rape ranked very high. About 5% of all the mental illnesses in the world were due to unknown causes and some could well have been purely biological origins (without trauma).

I was not only in shock to find this out, but I had to rethink about the way I think about mental illness. Why? Because if we lived in a better world where some people don't go around raping women or traumatizing children or bullying others, maybe we would not have mental illness, at least not as much as we have today. If mental illness is caused mostly by trauma, and especially childhood trauma, I had to work out a rational explanation for this. So, I did, together with my psychologist Bob Rich, PhD, who has been a therapist for decades.

- People vary in every way possible. All of us have genetic strengths and weaknesses. A weakness is only a potential, not a life sentence. For example, a genetic weakness to alcoholism will only be a problem for a person who abuses alcohol. Someone who drinks moderately, if at all, will never become an alcoholic. A person with a weak pancreas will probably avoid diabetes by keeping to an appropriate diet.

- Some genetic weaknesses predispose a person to a given kind of mental suffering, such as anxiety, depression, schizophrenia, etc. Again, these are not preordained problems, but are risks that manifest in specific circumstances.

- Early childhood experiences either provide protection from genetic weaknesses or trigger them. For example, a person who early on develops negative views of self would suffer from either depression or anxiety in adulthood. Which one of these manifests will depend on the presence of the relevant genetic weakness.

- Children who have inherited a tendency to develop a psychological problem are likely to be cared for by people with the same weakness. Therefore, early childhood experiences are likely to combine with genetic weaknesses rather than to protect against them. For this reason, there is not much point in worrying about genetics. You can't change your kids' genes, but you can change how you bring them up.

- A separate issue is resilience. This is the ability to stand up to stress, survive difficulties and thrive on challenges. It may also have a genetic basis. That is, some people may be naturally more robust than others.

- However, resilience changes over one's life span. It varies from time to time, situation to situation and is affected by things like current physical health, the thoughts going through your mind and the company you keep.

- At any one time, you are under a certain amount of stress. Its source doesn't matter that much. You can be stressed by work demands, life changes (even good ones), fatigue, illness, pain, conflict, grief, disappointment...all of these add up.

Stress can act like the irritants that precede an allergic reaction: accumulate enough of them and the mind and body react as if under attack.

- If the level of stress at this moment exceeds your resilience, then you will break. This break may be temporary or long-lasting, depending on many factors, including your thoughts about it.

Now we return to the beginning. When you break, the symptoms will be those determined by your genetic weaknesses and early childhood upbringing. People who suffer will respond to different treatments: placebo, medication or therapy—and for some others, nothing will help. We are up against a big problem. However, if children and adults were not traumatized by other people, the number of mental illness cases would minimal.

These are my ideas on the nature and causes of what we call mental illness. Having said this, I will now describe how I help people with mental illness using music, starting with bipolar disorder, which was once called manic depression.

4 Bipolar Disorder and Music Therapy

The advantage I have is that I suffer with bipolar II disorder, which is a milder form than my wife's bipolar I disorder. In my 2018 book, *Got Bipolar?* I wrote about the different types of bipolar disorders in terms of severity and differences in symptoms.

Broadly speaking, there are three types of bipolar disorder that can be distinguished by severity, manifestation and duration of symptoms. While bipolar I, bipolar II and cyclothymia are all characterized by alternating feelings of being high and being low, they differ.

Bipolar I disorder, or bipolar I (previously known as manic depression)—characterized by episodes of mania and deep depression—is the most severe. If not controlled, the feeling of being high can escalate into mania, where the person is unable to sleep, becomes irritable, experiences a rapid flow of ideas, speaks very quickly and tries to communicate everything at once (the result is a word salad of ideas). Also typical is irrational behavior, like spending money unwisely or risky sexual contacts. That is why this more severe condition of bipolar has often been mistakenly diagnosed as schizophrenia.

Bipolar II disorder, or bipolar II, is different from bipolar I in that there is no mania. Elevated moods can still cause problems, and deep depression is also present, but the highs never escalate into mania. Still, in bipolar II, a person who is experiencing elevated moods can suffer with serious problems, and sometimes they may also need hospitalization. Most of the symptoms of bipolar I are still present: pressured speech, distorted thinking, not sleeping, rapid flow of ideas, irritability and an inability to get along with people may all occur. These symptoms and moods do not go away in recovery, at least not completely. The person learns to live well despite the symptoms, which become accepted parts of the person's life.

Cyclothymia is the mildest of the three types. It is often called "bipolar light" in America and is characterized by frequent alternating moods, from highs to lows, sometimes within the same day. This milder form of highs and lows can be troublesome, as the moods and symptoms change rapidly. It is like riding a rollercoaster of moods, emotions and feelings. People with cyclothymia, more so than those with bipolar I or II, may often be driven to excessive alcohol or drug consumption, mostly to cope with the constant changing moods. No matter how serious your particular type of bipolar is, there is always hope. Having said this, we now turn to how music therapy can assist people with bipolar.

Music can help people with mental illness to find their own way out of the stigma and the symptoms often associated with a mental illness. While our society is still very ignorant when it comes to mental illness, for a variety of complicated reasons that I have expressed in my book, *Alfredo's Journey: An Artist's Creative Life With Bipolar Disorder* (2014), music can help us to express our suffering and, in doing so, help us to unload the great burden of ideas and emotions we carry with us. Expressing one's frustration is extremely important for recovery, which is why I strongly believe that therapy can truly assist in the recovery process.

Being part of the music world in any way—be it playing an instrument, simply listening or singing along—can help us to move the focus away from illness and toward imagination and creativity. This can help us gain a new, happier identity. Music is like a language that expresses our emotions. Even when we listen, we vicariously enter into the world of the performer and identify with the words he or she is singing. This is the transformation I want to explore. I am not the only one to feel this way; indeed, many other writers have argued along similar lines (e.g. Prateeksha Sharma, 2014).

Even if you don't play an instrument, you can certainly listen to music. There is lots of music out there, but the trick is to find songs or melodies that make you feel good, help you release emotions, and even cry. Music can elicit powerful emotions, which are very important for people with bipolar disorder.

This is important, because crying is like releasing a valve so that all bottled up emotions and problems may start to come out gradually. It will happen sooner or later. Getting rid of bottled-up negative emotions is a very important thing for recovery.

First of all, it is sometimes good to listen to sad songs, because we need to identify with them and so share our pain. This is contrary to what research indicates, because it can be dangerous in that the sufferer can possibly become even more depressed. However, given that I am aware of this problem, and that when I do it I keep in constant touch with the sufferer and am ready to suggest to discontinue should it become too strenuous, I have done this successfully so far. My suggestion is to try some sad songs to release emotions but to discontinue this if it becomes too stressful.

I may move onto songs of hope and encouragement. For example, Michael Bublé's song, "Dream," often gives me hope, particularly the part "...things are not as bad as they seem..." and those that encourage us fight to overcome the many unfair challenges of life. Words are important and, in the background, the brain can still pick up words and music even if we are busy, or thinking of other things. This is because the right song, played at the right level, does something to our inner self at a subconscious level. These songs get to our heart intelligence and help our spirit by providing some relief.

Here is a list of romantic songs I listen to.

- "Boulevard of Broken Dreams" (Dubin & Warren, 1933) [recorded by Diana Krall, 1996]

- "Desperado" (Frey & Henley, 1973) [recorded by The Eagles]

- "This Masquerade" (Leon Russel, 1972) [recorded by George Benson, 1976]

- "Dream" (Johnny Mercer, 1944) (recorded by Michael Bublé, 2007)

- "Always On My Mind" (Carson, Christopher and James, 1970) [recorded by Michael Bublé, 2007)

- "The Very Thought of You" (Ray Noble, 1934) [recorded by Nat King Cole, 1958]. This can be a friend or someone who supports us and helps us—even an email friend.

- "Home" (Michael Bublé, 2005)

- "Unforgettable" (Gordon and Gillette, 1951) [recorded by Nat King Cole, 1952]

- "They Can't Take That Away From Me" (George and Ira Gershwin, 1937)

This may seem an odd selection. These songs contain harmonies and words that are sung in such a beautiful manner that they will often bring up some emotions, but you may identify your pain with the singers who sing your favorite songs and they will give you hope to carry on.

These songs may not be ideal for everyone, but the structure is the same. It is good to start with a song sung by an artist who sings about misery and depression, because that is how we feel inside and many people with bipolar do feel this way as part of their mood cycles. You may share your pain with the singers and possibly cry or release some negative emotions, then gradually move on to songs of hope that still highlight the struggles of life and our suffering, but which lead to hope...things are not as bad as they seem...as in the song "Dreams."

For those situations where lyrical content is unwanted, I have assembled a series of classical-style piano tracks. These are available as MP3 files on my website www.AlfredoZotti.org/music-therapy and can be freely downloaded and stored in iTunes for your iPhone, computer, or other portable device.

If you need to hear the music at an increased volume, you can, but don't have it too loud or the effect on the inner self will be lost. Finally, there is no set rule. It is good to find the right songs for us that relieve depression. It takes a bit of research and experimentation, but once we find the songs they will help us for years to come. They will become our private little music collection to help us through the hardest times. Words, when coupled with music, take on a different meaning that has an effect on our psyche. Listening to words like, "...dream when you're feeling blue..." may help us in a way we did not think possible.

While it is important to stay away from music and words that describe despair, oblivion, tragedy, deep traumatic events and complete hopelessness, some sufferers like me have benefited from sad lyrics and songs giving an indication of how much of a mixed bag mental illness is. Of course, there is no precise way to select songs. Generally speaking it is a good idea to stay away from sad content in songs and music unless there is some evidence that this may help the sufferers.

iTunes and Windows Media Player and other apps are ideal for you to collect songs and listen to them when you need music to help you. My wife, Cheryl, suffers with bipolar I, and she began to create her own music library a few years ago. This is what she writes about listening to songs and singing along:

> My husband and I were living in a complex of houses where some individuals were making life miserable for others. Many were on drugs and there were fights, arguments and a lot of evil in the complex. Most of the people there were highly stressed due to noise at night. My heart specialist, who was taking care of my high blood pressure and chronic headaches at the time, advised me to take up a hobby so that I could better cope with all of that. I decided to listen to music and to sing along with it. My husband, who is a musician, agreed with the doctor's suggestion and helped me to create a little library of songs using an old iMac G3 as a jukebox.
>
> Soon, I discovered that I could easily lose myself in the music and sing in the mornings, which would help me all through the day. The problem that we were having with our troubled neighbors soon seemed less of a burden, and I could now cope better. I continued to sing, and as I did I got stronger, I got better and felt that I now had a strong identity of a woman that loved music and who loved to sing along to the beautiful songs. To complement my music, I had made a beautiful garden at the front of our little two-story cottage.
>
> Soon, I discovered that singing along with the songs was helping me with other difficulties, such as my bipolar disorder. Admittedly, when I became depressed, occasionally I would stop listening to the music. But this was OK, because I knew that soon I would return to listening and singing along. There is no doubt that music has helped me get through some of the most difficult periods in my life. Now, at 70 years of age, I realize that singing is also helping my memory, as I remember all of the lyrics of the songs, and I feel that music in general is helping me to stay well, to stay positive and to look on the bright side of life.

One of the most important things that my wife mentioned is that she gained a kind of identity away from the usual ill person who is trapped in negativity and suffering. As my wife writes, she now had an identity—she was the lady who sung along to some beautiful songs and felt really good while doing it. She could tell all her friends and family members about it, and I can see how this did give her a strong sense of who she was. It is important to have a strong identity that one can rely on. It can truly help us in difficult times.

My story is pretty similar in terms of identity. I am a musician, a piano player, songwriter and composer. I play a number of musical instruments, including piano, drums, bass and guitar. My main instrument is the piano. Music has given me a strong identity, because I am a well-respected musician. This has helped tremendously in giving me hope and confidence and the ability to know that when depression or elevated moods come, they are part of my artistic personality, and, as such, I know that these troublesome moods will eventually pass. Finding a hobby or a passion or a job that one loves is important for people with bipolar disorder, for it can give them a strong identity—particularly if they are good at what they do.

As years go by, I become better at copying with various symptoms and moods, and now I am at a stage in my life where I function well, even when my bipolar is active. I have learned to control my bipolar disorder so that it does not disrupt my life. This has been possible precisely because of my music. It does not mean that there will be no more episodes where I am unwell, but it does mean that I am pretty stable and able to enjoy life.

During depression, which is a main symptom of bipolar disorder, people may not feel like listening to music, preferring quietness because depression is a very debilitating condition. It is just like some don't listen to music when in chronic pain. However, being a musician, I am often forced to play and listen to music when I am depressed. I must say that this helps tremendously, even if it is a great effort in the initial stages. When I am depressed and have to play music, the situation changes immediately after my hands touch an instrument or I listen to a good music piece. Therefore, I think that for future research, it would be important to look into the benefits of forcing oneself to play an instrument or listening to music when depressed. This makes sense in that music makes us happy and has an effect on our brain. Research has shown that cracking a smile in front of a mirror, when depressed, releases endorphins in the body and these help us to feel better. (BeyondBlue.org.au, 2020)

Music is powerful and can positively affect people's mental health. It can arouse strong emotions in listeners (Vastfjall, 2002). Music can bring about feelings of peace and calmness and can be a diversion from the monotony and harshness of everyday life (Bednarz & Nikkel, 1992). Bednarz and Nikkel's work indicates that music does improve the life of people with mental illness. Their research was based on five main interventions: music instructions, music discussion, expressive music intervention, group participatory music and music listening.

One of the most important ways that music can have a positive impact on people with mental illness is that it can affect mood— either positively or negatively—and this is why the presence of a music therapist is important. For example, some music can lead to neurosis or anxiety, and some lyrics can promote suicidal ideation and even suicide itself. Different music genres can affect people in different ways, especially children and teens. Listening to happy or angry music can affect emotions and thus contribute to highs and lows. The type of music that one listens to has a bearing on mood. Some studies have shown that listening to some classical music can induce a sense of peace and calm, while listening to heavy metal can elicit tension and anxiety (Rea, et al., 2010).

Contrasting emotional responses emerge from listening to diverse forms of music. Because of the many factors involved, you need a music therapist to identify the ideal music for you at this time (Peters, 2000).

Music is also about lyrical content, which is important when considering music's impact on children and adolescents. Daniel Västfjäll makes note of "the importance of considering the content of lyrics and its effect on mood." Emotions are also important, and music can help a person with emotional problems, particularly those that have no family or are homeless and therefore lack an emotional attachment (Västfjäll, D. 2002 p. 26).

David Simonelli, associate professor of history at Youngstown State University, argues that punk rock is a "revitalizing element that perfectly captured youth anger" (Simonelli, 2013. p. xix).

Based on existing studies, music therapy can be one effective, non-invasive way to improve mental health, and positive changes in music habits may positively affect symptoms of depression and bipolar disorder.

In *Music and Mind in Everyday Life*, Sheffield, Clarke, Dibben and Pitts state that music is "a means for people to alter their mood," and also a means to achieve a "desired emotional state" (Sheffield et al, 2012, p. 90).

Some choose music that allows them to "ruminate" more deeply in a negative emotion, while others choose music that helps them achieve a more positive emotional state, according to the authors.

Discerning choices in quantity and type of music can be one factor in achieving greater mood stability and in self-regulation for bipolar disorder. Parents should be aware of how music may affect their children's mood and both educate and regulate their child's or teen's music habits. This principle can also be applied to policies in public schools and in educating youth in habits contributing to improved mental health (Simonelly, 2013; Lanham, 2012; Clark, et al., 2009).

Case Study: Mark / Bipolar I

I began to help Mark in the year 2012, and we have remained friends since then. Mark suffers with bipolar I disorder. I started to help him using music at a time when he could hardly cope and was contemplating suicide.

Every case is different, and as a music therapist, I know that my aim is always to find a music program specifically tailored to each person. In this sense, the music program should be unique. In Mark's case, I realized that he had a lot of bottled-up issues, and I had to help him release some. I had to help him to find a way to cry, to open the valve that would free some of the dangerous emotions that he had bottled up inside. For this, and this is not usual in that using sad music can at times be dangerous, I did use sad music, music that made Mark cry. But during this time, I was close to him, keeping in constant communication. I was Mark's support for a while until I helped him to create his own support network.

Initially, I tried to guess what kind of songs appealed to Mark. So, I suggested Billy Joel's "Summer Highland Falls." I never anticipated that Mark would fall in love with this song, just as I had many years ago when I first learned about my bipolar disorder. This song really touched a note in Mark's mind. As he told me, he had it on repeatedly for a full day, non-stop. What he really loved was the phrase, "Now we are forced to recognize our inhumanity. A reason coexists for our insanity." Mark told me he had learned from both this song and me that bipolar had a purpose in his life and that was to create, for he was also a highly creative person. Incidentally, since we are here discussing creativity, it is a fact that the proportion of creative people is much higher in the bipolar population compared to the normal population. (Jamison, 2014).

The second song I gave him was kind of really sad but it was something with which he could identify, and I thought it was important for him to know that others have felt the same way, have walked the same road. "Boulevard of Broken Dreams," as Mark told me, really opened up the tap of his tears as he started to cry profusely. This is what I wanted to do, to make sure Mark cried. At the same time, I told him he could call me day and night and had been transparent with him warning him that this song may well bring out overwhelming emotions but not to distress too much as this was going to be a process that would lead to better health and state of mind. I think he believed me, and I was with him all through this process. It was not easy for me either, but I knew it had to be done.

This was how Mark was feeling for a long time, alienated and excluded by stigma. Now, he could cry about it and let all of the associated emotions out. After this particular song had done its job, and as Mark tells me he still listens to it occasionally when he is in the right mood for it, we moved onto happier songs. The next song was "Eye of the Tiger," performed by Survivor (2008). The lyrics speak for themselves. Mark loved it, and, as he told me, it gave him lots of courage and strength to carry on. I made sure to tell Mark to pay attention to the words, to study the words, because many people don't often pay attention to the lyrics. Lyrics are very important.

I hope that this example about Mark clearly brings home the idea that music can truly help in a very powerful way. Later on, I'll discuss depression. Of course, many things that have been said in this chapter are also valid for any mental illness, but little variations are important. For depression, a much bigger effort is required to help people with music therapy, since many people in the grip of deep depression do not like to listen to any music.

5 | Autism Spectrum Disorder and Music Therapy

What is autism? Does music really help people with autism? I shall explore these two questions in this chapter. Autism spectrum disorder is a very broad term used to describe a group of neurodevelopmental disorders. The main characteristics of these disorders are poor or inadequate communication and social interaction. In addition, people with autism show restricted, repetitive, and stereotyped interests or patterns of behavior (Legg, 2018).

Until recently, there has been no scientific evidence in support of the idea that music benefits people with autism, and therapists have relied on everyday practical observation. However, some studies have shown that music therapy is conducive to improvements in social communication and auditory-motor connectivity in children with autism, particularly thanks to fMRI scans and advanced technology in neuroscience (Sharda et al., 2018).

The Diagnostic and Statistical Manual of Mental Disorders (DSM–V) currently recognizes five different dimensions of autism spectrum disorder, which are:

- With or without accompanying intellectual impairment

- With or without accompanying language impairment

- Associated with a known medical or genetic condition or environmental factor

- Associated with another neurodevelopmental, mental or behavioral disorder

- With catatonia

Prior to the DSM-V, diagnosis was based on the choice of one of the following disorders:

- Autistic disorder

- Asperger's syndrome

- Pervasive developmental disorder not otherwise specified (PDD-NOS)

- Childhood disintegrative disorder

Once a diagnosis is made from one of the above disorder classifications, a person does not need to be reevaluated. The diagnosis is permanent and final (Legg, 2018).

Autism usually becomes evident from early childhood, between 12 and 24 months of age. Nevertheless, symptoms can also appear later or earlier. One of the most obvious symptoms is a marked delay in language and/or social development. According to the DSM-5, there are two major distinctions: problems with communication and social interaction; and restricted or repetitive patterns of behavior or activities.

For a diagnosis of autism spectrum disorder (ASD), a person must display all three symptoms in the first category and at least two symptoms in the second category. Having said this, if your child is experiencing problems that disrupt daily routine, it is important to seek immediate help. No matter what may be wrong with your child, even if it is not autism but some other developmental problem, early intervention is important. If the problems are attended to in the early stages, chances are that your child will improve and find a way to cope with life (Smith et al., 2019).

Teaching music to autistic children is a great challenge because they have problems with social interactions and focusing attention. It is important for the therapist to find out as much as possible about the child and make every attempt to create a personalized musical treatment plan. It is also important to listen to the parents' ideas, hopes and challenges. Parents can be very stressed and find it very challenging caring for a child with autism, and it is not uncommon to find them to be depressed, anxious and disappointed with the educational or medical system.

As a music teacher to many autistic children, I have developed my own method over the years. My philosophy is based on the idea that any problems I have with the child are due to my failings as a teacher. Rather than beat myself up, my task is to find a way to make things work, changing my approach and becoming more aware of the nonverbal signals the child uses to communicate their frustration, feelings, desires and discomfort. This philosophy has paid off time and time again.

I am proud of the fact that today many music therapists often contact me to ask how to create a cooperative environment for the autistic child so that learning and teaching can be maximized. I have made many music therapist and psychologist friends, because I help people as a volunteer online, and because I am interested in music therapy.

When I teach a child with autism, I treat each one as an individual with his/her own unique needs and abilities. When an autistic child comes to me for the first time, and we go to my music room, I don't have a preconceived lesson plan. This comes later, after many sessions, when we cooperate to structure the lessons. In the beginning, I let the child decide what to do, and he/she usually tells me this in different ways, such as nonverbal facial expressions and behavior that I have learned to read over the years. For this to happen, the music room must be colorful and have lots of interesting things (instruments, a computer, etc.)

For example, Colin first came to me when he was 6 years of age. He was nonverbal and extremely shy. I could immediately read his mum's face: she had very little trust in me and probably thought that I would fail miserably, and that she would have to leave with the child screaming in tears and me stressed out. True, this could have certainly happened if I hadn't had experience. But the child came into my room, and we both sat on chairs. The computer was on, and I had a nice, colorful program with which I was writing music. I purposely left it on, for I thought that this might capture his attention. But I also had other things, like little musical instruments (a harmonica, an accordion, a flute, a clarinet, a tambourine) everywhere.

After a few minutes of silence, as we were sitting in the chairs, I noticed the child looking very interested at the computer screen. Without saying a word, I touched the mouse and started pointing at the different music notations that were now changing colors as the mouse pointer passed over the notes. I sensed that the child wanted to use the mouse, so I made a gesture that indicated that he could pick up the mouse and drive it. So, he took control of the mouse and started to click over the notes. From there, I started to explain to him what a crotchet is, what a semiquaver is, what a treble clef is or a bass clef. His interest was clearly noted, and so that was our way to start to learn music. It was the child who told me how he wanted to start, what he wanted to do and how he would easily learn music. This was ideal for starting a relationship between child and teacher. It is precisely how autistic children learn and come to trust—by doing things, not by talking or being told. We can forget words in the initial stages, but need to rely on other types of communication, and I believe that this is an extremely important point for music therapists.

From that day forward, we used the computer to specifically learn piano and to generally learn about music. After many weeks, the computer was eliminated and the child was now a little piano player, certainly better than many musicians around today. Because autistic children often have natural abilities, this particular child could imitate almost anything he heard. The only limiting factor was his finger technique.

What I want to highlight in this example is that I don't tell children what to do in the first lesson; rather, I wait till they show me how they would like to begin to learn music. I am going to repeat it here because it is vital: for an optimal learning environment, there needs to be an adequate variety of things from which the child can learn. This can be colored music books, a variety of little and big musical instruments, computer programs or anything to do with music that may capture the attention and interest of the child. For a child with autism, there is nothing worse than forcefully telling him/her what to do, making learning feel like hard work and making the lessons boring. This is not adequate, and unfortunately, this is a mistake that many music therapists often make.

For a music teacher, it is vital to pay attention to the child's sensory sensitivities. Some children are sensitive to sound, to light, to touch, taste or smell, and these sensory perceptions are important. During the lesson, making time for fun and ensuring that there is room for a smile, for a laugh or for any sign of feeling good and happy is important. As I mentioned before, nonverbal cues are essential. Autistic children are good at communicating with nonverbal cues, and it is important for the teacher to learn to decipher these signals. It is important to consider the fact that many children with autism do not often use gestures and they seldom, if ever, make eye contact. Such behavior may make them seem uninterested. But they will have little outbursts making strange or unusual sounds with their vocal chords or have an unusual look on their faces or show subtle and unusual behavior. By unusual behavior

I mean repetitive behavior, such as flapping hands or wrists for self-soothing and other tics, like you would see with Tourette syndrome, are often present.

A good music therapist will learn to read the unusual behavior, no matter how insignificant or strange it may seem to a person. The therapist will take action according to what he/she thinks the child would want to say but is unable to communicate. Sometimes, it is pure intuition. That is why women make the best music therapists, because women have developed intuition due to their genetic motherly tendencies. But some men are also sensitive and have developed intuition. I am fortunate in that way.

Consistency and routine are of the utmost importance. Children with ASD do best when they have structured schedules and routines. If there is an unavoidable schedule change, it is important to try to prepare the child for it in advance.

How Does Music Help Children With Autism?

It is only within the past decade that some research has shed light on the effects of music on the autistic brain. (Schellenberg et al., 2015). Prior to these research studies, we only had observational evidence—no scientific evidence. That music has therapeutic properties on the minds of humans was something well known since the times of Plato. Now, with some scientific research backing what we have always known in a practical sense, the case for music therapy is stronger than ever, and I hope that one day soon governments around the world begin to sponsor music therapy and offer it to poor people and children who cannot afford it. This is because where medicine fails, particularly in autism, music therapy can make all of the difference.

One of the reasons that music has become a reliable tool in autism therapy is because it stimulates both sides of the brain (Sharda et al., 2018). Music encourages communication and social interaction, even among children with autism. As I have already discussed, the brain is plastic, and music therapy is certainly something that works on the plasticity of the brain to bring about better social and motor skills. Playing a musical instrument will mean that the autistic child begins to interact with the instrument at first and slowly moves to interact with others through the music. Thus, a new word may be learned from a song, or the child is helped to understand how to behave in certain situations that are suggested by appropriate song lyrics.

Dancing can also help to stimulate sensory systems and enhance motor skills.

For example, I began to teach the piano to a child with severe autism with intellectual impairment. I remember the first lesson. When the child came to my study room where I have my piano, I could sense he was very nervous and unsure as to what to do. I knew the child could sense that I was at ease with him in that I have been dealing with autistic children for a number of years, and therefore I can read silent cues and facial expression that are very subtle and difficult to identify.

Bob sat in the chair and I simply began to play the piano, but I made sure to play some of the most beautiful movie themes. Immediately, I sensed that the child was captured in the moment, listening attentively to the music, looking closely at what I was doing, pressing the many black and white keys and making all sorts of different movements with my hands. I could have started to talk during the lesson but this would have proved totally inadequate as the child would have switched off and gone into his own internal world, paying absolutely no attention to me. But listening to the music and watching me play was different, something he had not seen before.

Needless to say, Bob fell in love with the piano. We started to play the scales, and then we moved to simple melodies. Just as for Alzheimer's, I began to write little tunes with lyrics that had special little instructions that Bob could use in his everyday life. For example, he had trouble brushing his teeth, and his mum was totally frustrated. After writing a special song about brushing one's teeth, and after both of us brushing our teeth in front of a mirror in the bathroom, Bob soon learned to enjoy brushing his teeth. His mum said he would sing the song, making the gestures of brushing, and then, after singing the song, he went to the bathroom to brush his teeth. This soon became a ritual. It is these things, combined with routine, that make all the difference for autistic children.

Bob's mum stated clearly that after beginning to play the piano and doing music therapy, Bob had improved tremendously and his life had improved. His attention span, his enthusiasm for things and his happiness…everything had changed for the better. This is the real power of music for children with autism, but there is also need for a gifted music teacher who does music therapy through real life. I am not a qualified music therapist, but I am a talented musician, arranger and composer, and I have lots of experience with disabilities—both on the personal and professional level. I maintain that therapists who have suffered directly with a mental disability make the best therapists, because they have hands on experience.

To conclude what has been highlighted in this short chapter, are these the facts:

- To begin to teach an autistic child, it is important to establish trust and let the child decide how to begin the teacher-student relationship in an environment of fun, discoveries and freedom...an environment where there is no room for hard work or regimental training but simply enjoyable learning that is free and fun.

- After a few lessons, the teacher can begin to bring structure to the lessons, but this must be done in cooperation with the student, and it is true that a certain friendship must be established between the teacher and the autistic child.

- Parents must be consulted and need to be part of the equation. They will need to be consulted at all levels of the teaching and even helped to continue on the success interventions of the music teacher at home.

- The teacher must never assume that the child represents a hopeless case. This is never the case in my experience. The teacher is always at fault, because there is always a way to teach all children.

- A music teacher must research the area that they are teaching: If it is autism, they should read widely about autism, including the latest research and discoveries. Searching for novel ways to maximize the learning is always an important, and the teacher should also consider him or herself an eternal student.

Girls with ASD Differ From Boys and Often Go Undiagnosed

I had been helping Mary online for a few months. She suffered with anxiety and depression, and, as she told me, this was due to the fact that her daughter was very shy, introverted and was having lots of trouble learning at school. When Mary told me this, and knowing that she was experiencing financial problems because she was divorced and her wages were barely paying rent and putting food on the table, I offered to teach her daughter, Linda, the piano, and told Mary that this could be great therapy for her daughter.

I remember the first lesson. The first thing that came to my mind was this: *What if this girl has autism and no one has yet diagnosed her?* Indeed, I could see several signs of autism in the behavior patterns of this 12-year-old girl. She was functioning, but with several serious problems. This presented a great dilemma, because on the one hand, I did not want to tell Mary, who was already suffering with anxiety; on the other hand, I am transparent in things, or at least I try to be, so that the best thing for me to do was to be honest with Linda's mother and tell her the truth.

I had seen this before and was aware that while it is fairly easy to diagnose boys, for complex reasons, girls seem to fall through the cracks and are often termed "lost girls" or "hiding in plain sight." Some girls are good at hiding the signs, at least while they are young. Even when presentation is clear, as it was in this case, autism in girls can be overlooked. The history Mary gave me included the fact that Linda had significant language delays, that she experienced frequent meltdowns and that it was difficult, as I came to see after a few lessons, for her to change routines that were not so efficient.

> The model that we have for a classic autism diagnosis has really turned out to be a male model. That's not to say that girls don't ever fit it, but girls tend to have a quieter presentation, with not necessarily as much of the repetitive and restricted behavior, or it shows up in a different way. Stereotypes may get in the way of recognition. So where the boys are looking at train schedules, girls might have excessive interest in horses or unicorns, which is not unexpected for girls. But the level of the interest might be missed and the level of oddity can be a little more damped down. It's not quite as obvious to an untrained eye. (Epstein in Arky, 2020).

This idea that diagnosing autism is predisposed to noting the typical behaviors of male children is in agreement with much research that calls for accurate diagnosis of ASD for both sexes and better understanding of gender differences. (Halladay et al., 2015; Werling & Geschwind, 2013). Other research has shown actual brain differences between boys and girls with ASD. (Lai at al., 2012).

Linda continues her lessons to this day, and I offer my services as a volunteer, because my music therapy makes a real difference in the lives of some young people. In the face of the fact that governments do not subsidize music therapy for poor people here in Australia, I think that there is a need for volunteers to fill the gap, because our young people need help. Volunteering to help young people with my music therapy has given me great knowledge about what can be done in our world.

After two years of piano lessons, Linda has changed for the better. This has given me evidence that the piano does wonders for the brain, as I have discussed elsewhere in this book. Because of her musical abilities, Linda is now more social, less isolated, has more friends and is much happier. She has formed a little band with some of her friends, and they play for fun. This, in turn, has improved the life of her mother, who no longer has anxiety or depression. By the way, I told her mum of my assessment, and because she is an educated lady, she fully understood me and knows I help other children with autism. She took no offence and was glad that I had told her. The future is bright, and if music can do this, then it is a valuable tool for ASD that governments should consider, because failure to provide early interventions can be very costly to governments in the long run because the people that are unwell are a burden on the health system, affecting family members and friends, and this is the domino effect of ill health.

6 Schizophrenia and Music Therapy

Before I begin to write about schizophrenia, which is a very complex topic, it is necessary to have a look at how schizophrenia is treated in first world countries, like America or Australia, and then move on to show how music therapy can be integrated into the interventions to help people with this diagnosis.

Psychiatrist Thomas Insel (2013, p. 26) writes,

> It appears that what we currently call "schizophrenia" may comprise disorders with quite different trajectories. For some people, remaining on medication long-term might impede a full return to wellness. For others, discontinuing medication can be disastrous.

Schizophrenia is not a uniform disorder that affects all sufferers in the same way. Each case is unique and the one-size-fits-all research, based on the biomedical model, does more harm than good.

Currently we need a medical model that embraces diversity, that embraces holism and that empowers sufferers. Unfortunately, we have a medical model that, driven by financial and political ideologies, fails to consider the complexities of schizophrenia. This is bad science.

While many researchers are careful not to use words that can appear derogatory or offensive to sufferers, they do little to ensure that sufferers are not disempowered, because research can have a disempowering, underlying message.

Focusing on the Negative Facts

A recent focus of investigation is acoustic research, particularly the mismatch negativity (MMN) model that relies on the complex understanding of event-related potential (ERP) and how this represents aspects of the sound environment of our brain. Todd et al., (2011) and Stoner et al., (2013), focusing on this sound environment, found that people with schizophrenia have reduced MMN amplitude compared to that of non-sufferers.

Studies are conducted in a laboratory environment where the sufferer is exposed to a chain of equal and repeated sounds that are occasionally disrupted by an unusual (oddball) sound that briefly interrupts the constant chain of sounds. The odd sound will be reintroduced, time and time again, at intervals. A normal brain picks up the oddball sounds, but the brain of a schizophrenic shows decreased performance in identifying (and predicting the coming of) the oddball sound.

What makes this research interesting is that the subject does not need to pay attention to the sounds, and, indeed, subjects can be watching a movie or reading a book during this experiment (Todd et al., 2011). The brain of the subject will record the sound differences even if the person is asleep or in a coma.

Researchers look at the neurobiology of schizophrenia and create a negative picture of sufferers whose intellect is impaired by their illness. It is well known that in some cases (but not all) the brains of people with schizophrenia undergo massive neural pruning. It can be seen on before and after images and is most evident in the expansion of the channels of the brain, in which fluid is found, in the central region. But we must ask ourselves: what is causing this massive deterioration? Is it the illness itself? Is it the lack of social support and understanding? Or is it the potent and toxic medication? Is it the withdrawal from social life? Or could it partly be our inability to empower people with schizophrenia so that they can help themselves live a reasonable life? Is it our stigma that makes these people sick? These are the sorts of questions that a researcher who values a holistic approach should ask. Indeed, it is well documented that, for many sufferers, it is not the voices or hallucinations that are the real problems as much as what other people think of their psychotic experiences (Corry & Tubridy, 2001).

These questions become even more interesting when we consider that some people with chronic schizophrenia function very well. They may have reduced amplitude in discriminating sound differences, picked up by MMN studies, but the intelligence of many sufferers seems to remain intact. Some people with schizophrenia are professors, like Elyn Saks, who is professor of law and a decorated academic and a great advocate for better mental health treatment of people with schizophrenia. There are many success stories of people with schizophrenia who have found a way to live well with their condition and can control it in such a way as to live a good life.

In addition to these success stories, I have been writing as an equal member on schizophrenia.com for a number of years. I don't suffer with schizophrenia, and I do not experience psychosis, but I am interested and have been studying schizophrenia for a number of years. Also, I am in communication with many sufferers with schizophrenia and this is perhaps the difference between my work and that of a researcher. My work is based on the attempt to befriend people with schizophrenia and really get to know them, their hopes, their abilities, their success stories and generally more of the positive stuff that researchers dismiss. In my longitudinal personal research, I have found many people with schizophrenia with reduced amplitude/perception but who still function well.

I know that there are thousands of high-functioning schizophrenics out there who are doctors, psychologists, academics, journalists, artists, musicians and actors. The success stories of these people don't seem to support the basic idea of MMN research in terms of presenting people with schizophrenia as being intellectually affected by the disorder in some very negative way. These people perform well and have been doing so for years.

Yet, research on MMN seems to portray schizophrenics negatively. Schizophrenia is presented as an illness that negatively affects people's intellect, and that a wonder drug will restore intellectual capacities as we wait for scientists to identify the genes responsible for this illness so that we can eradicate it.

For now, a lot of research indicates that antipsychotics may be the cause of such brain deterioration seen in schizophrenia (e.g., Salisbury et al., 2002). Indeed, Salisbury et al. found that first episode schizophrenia shows similar MMN tests results to those of normal people. Reduced amplitude is not noted in first episode schizophrenics. However, marked amplitude is noted in people who have already endured multiple episodes or who are heavily medicated chronic sufferers.

If we look at the situation differently, from a more holistic perspective, we may begin to ponder on the possibility that for some schizophrenics, it is the "software" that is the real problem, not the "hardware" or the way in which they perceive the world. As we have seen, some sufferers are able to change their perception with their own mind. Once the software is fixed, the hardware begins to work well, even if there are some deficiencies.

The Open Dialogue Approach

The "Open Dialogue" is a Finnish approach to treating *first-break psychosis*, particularly in younger people. It was devised and introduced by a group of family therapists of Tornio, Finland, at the Keropudas Hospital.

They have been able to change what was once one of the poorest outcomes for schizophrenia in the whole of Europe into a successful way to help sufferers to recover, often permanently. The method has worked time and again, over many years, and many research studies have been conducted with promising outcomes for first-break schizophrenia. The aim is to avoid hospitalization and administration of drugs (early interventions) and to help people recover so that they are able to work and get back to their lives. By treating schizophrenia in its earliest stages, they have greatly reduced rates of hospitalization and minimized the need for drugs. Such positive outcomes have captured the attention of many mental health professionals who are dissatisfied with the Western system of treating people with hospitalizations and administration of neuroleptics, which can make things worse in the long run.

The Finnish family therapists work in groups, because they see psychosis as a problem that involves relationships. The treatment is based on an open dialogue to find the best treatment for each person. Family and friends are a vital part of this treatment, where medication and other problems are discussed openly. The therapists can be a selection from among a psychiatric nurse, a psychiatrist, a psychologist and a family therapist. Working in teams of mental health experts from various disciplines makes the treatment more powerful, and this is something that we will consider closely as I discuss the freely available online film that was presented by therapist, musician and filmmaker, Daniel Mackler. There is no doubt that this incredibly effective method promotes medication-free recovery, while offering evidence that can be used to critique contemporary psychiatry. Of course, this does not mean that the open dialogue method belongs to the anti-psychiatry movement. Indeed, the Finnish team does rely on a psychiatrist to lead. Mackler's film, "Open Dialogue: an alternative Finnish approach to healing psychosis" is available at www.alfredozotti.org/music-therapy.

One of the biggest critics of this method is Marvin Ross (2013), who states that we need further research to see if such a method can be used outside Finland. That's ridiculous. There is nothing country-specific in such an approach. It has been successfully used on other issues within the family therapy tradition for many years. Ross then writes that, "A 'filmmaker' produced the video on open dialogue." This "filmmaker" was a practicing therapist who decided to become a musician and filmmaker, perhaps due to having lost hope in traditional Western ways of treating people with mental disorders. Ross goes on to write, as Dr. Olsen argues (2014),

> ...that when one looks closely at the research, the Open Dialogue method does not really have better results than our current method of early interventions which, in the medical book *The Merck Manual*, is stated to be at around 30%.

In other words, the early interventions of Western societies show a recovery from first episode schizophrenia of 30%. Dr. Olsen (2014) states that statistics show that we are now well below the 30% recovery mark when it comes to psychosis and gradually losing ground. For example, Wunderink et al., (2013) give us only 17.6% recovery rates of those who had received standard care for a first time psychotic episode, while Harrow (2007) found that only 5% of sufferers recovered with standard care. It is evident now that Ross' idea that the open dialogue results are not different from our outcomes in the Western world is based on a false premise.

We do not have 30% recovery of first time psychotic episodes in the Western world, simply because our practice is to restrain the person who is experiencing psychosis, take him/her to the hospital and administer neuroleptic drugs. Having said this, let's now take a look at how, simply by listening to music, music therapy can assist people with schizophrenia to improve their symptoms.

Music Therapy for Schizophrenia and Psychosis

Between 60 and 80% of patients with schizophrenia experience auditory hallucinations, and these, in turn, have been linked to great levels of anxiety and severe depression (Pinar, 2018). Despite receiving anti-psychotic drugs, about 50% of patients continue to experience hallucinations, and this is a serious problem in that hallucinations can lead to self-harm and sometimes harming others (Andrew, 2010). Psycho-social techniques have been proven effective. including music therapy (ibid).

In 2018, a longitudinal study showed that patients subjected to music interventions, compared to the no music intervention control group, demonstrated improved functional connectivity in the *dorsal anterior insula* area of the brain and *posterior insula* networks. After just one month of music therapy treatment, the patients showed marked improvement, which was observed thanks to magnetic resonance imaging, or fMRI scans (He et al., 2018).

Other studies, such as De Sousa & De Sousa's (2010) *Music Therapy in Chronic Schizophrenia*, show that music therapy can be used in conjunction with medication. In this particular study on 272 patients with chronic schizophrenia, results indicated that music therapy may prove an effective tool in the holistic rehabilitation of people with schizophrenia as an adjunct to various pharmacotherapy and psychosocial treatments.

In Finland, music therapy is used, with good results, at all stages of schizophrenia, showing that music controls psychosis by reducing symptoms. In his chapter, Naukkarinen (1984) discusses the importance of music in therapy and also the importance of early interventions.

Sismey and Gillett (2015 p. 18) write about the implications of music therapy for schizophrenia:

> Music therapy can help people with schizophrenia improve their global state and the negative symptoms of schizophrenia. Clinicians would be justified in offering music therapy over the short term to medium term. However, effects of music therapy seem to be heavily dependent on the number of music therapy sessions... Difficult to predict how many sessions individual patients will need.

This idea is supported by writers such as Anderson (2019), who writes that "listening to music appears to reduce the need for medication to treat agitation in psychiatric inpatients."

Case Study: Sandra's Psychotic Episodes

As an online helper, I have had the opportunity to help people, using music therapy, with mild to moderate schizophrenia. Sandra suffers with psychosis and her psychotic episodes could happen anywhere at any time. She is one of the rare sufferers who is aware of having hallucinations—when they start and when they end. Not all sufferers with schizrenia are aware that what they perceive is not real, but Maria was one of the lucky ones, and this means that it is much easier for her to recover. It is true to say that because of my limitations, I can only be of assistance to people who are fairly aware of their condition and symptoms.

During our conversations, she told me that she was terrified, because when a psychotic episode happened, she would be totally taken into this kind of strange world where everyone was against her and she felt sick and frightened. Faces and voices would come to her and she would become completely terrified, because many of the voices were truly cruel and nasty and would say terrible things. One day, I got a message on my phone, although we usually communicate either via messenger of Skype. The message was: "Please help me, I am in a shopping center, and I have locked myself in the washroom, but I cannot escape the voices."

I quickly replied that if there was music that could be heard in the washroom, given that all shopping centers have music, to focus on that or alternatively to go out in the shopping center, even if this was unpleasant initially, to find a seat, sit down and focus on the music; try to focus hard on the music, listen to it attentively.

After a few hours, I received another message that while Sandra could hear no music from the washroom, she went out into the shopping center, found a seat, focused on the Barry Manilow music playing and that this helped her to get out of the psychotic episode. I was truly surprised how well this worked. We can learn several things from this example. I think that most of the problem is how people respond to schizophrenia sufferers. If we make a big deal about the experience of psychosis, it is likely that the sufferers will feel much worse, as we are passing on to them our prejudice, ignorance and unkindness.

If we treat the psychosis as a problem that can be overcome and treat it as part of life—as something that can be worked upon and helped—then the sufferer is much more likely to feel they have a friend in us, someone they can trust and count on and their psyche will respond positively. It does count if the sufferer likes the music. This makes the effects of music more powerful.

In my attempt to help suffers with schizophrenia online, using music therapy, I have devised the following method, which seems to work well for all of them. In the initial stages, there is always tension between therapist/helper and sufferers and this can only be overcome by honesty and transparency.

I start by telling the sufferer, "Before I begin to help you, you should know that I do not suffer with psychosis, but by helping others with psychosis for a few years, I have come to understand the situation."

What we call schizophrenia is best described by Corry and Tubridy (2001, p. 35), who write,

> Schizophrenia is a psychotic mental disorder characterized by a breakdown in the relationship between thoughts, feelings and actions, usually accompanied by withdrawal from social activity and the occurrence of delusions and hallucinations... Psychosis is a severe mental illness or disorder involving a loss of contact with reality frequently with hallucinations and delusions or altered thought processes. Hallucination is the apparent perception of an external object or sensory input when no such object or stimulus is present (seeing things, hearing voices). Delusion is a false impression or opinion not shared by others.

The nearest I have come to experiencing this is when I dream. When I dream, I also see things that aren't there, and I can even have experiences in the dream that seem very real, like having sex or being terrified and so on. In other words, I believe that psychosis is a bit like dreaming, only psychosis happens when people are awake. For example, when I dream, I am next to my wife, and yet she does not see or experience the things I see in dreams. In this sense, we all have potential for psychosis and to experience psychosis. While the dream ends when the alarm bell rings or when we wake up in the morning, psychosis in a person with schizophrenia is continuous (recurring) and happens during the day.

It is widely known that the onset of schizophrenia is not sudden. It happens slowly and gradually and "is an integral part and experience of the person's life history. It is a process rather than a sudden event."(Corry and Trubridy, 2001, p.46). Also, it is a fact that people with schizophrenia are socially isolated, avoid crowds, are alienated and often bullied because of being different and often are obviously different. The problem is how to find a way in which the sufferer can learn coping skills that make it possible to live at peace and find a way to bridge the internal world of a schizophrenic with the reality of the external world. Being aware is a great plus towards recovery as I have already written, but even for those who know about their condition, because a health specialist has told them or because they have become aware due to being different, there is always help. We must remember that mystics and schizophrenics share the same ocean but that mystics swim well and thrive while schizophrenics often drown. There is a way to ensure that people with schizophrenia learn to swim, and this is what I try to do when I help people. In other words, I do not see schizophrenics as people who cannot be helped, but, rather, who can do great things in life thanks to their different ways of perception and action.

Once I tell this to sufferers, they usually take a few days to think about it. The great majority will come back to me, and this means that the barrier has been broken, that they trust me now and they understand that I do have some understanding of their condition. One of the biggest mistakes is to underestimate the intelligence that I have found in people with schizophrenia and also their great creativity and ability to see things from novel perspectives. These qualities, if tapped into, can lead to recovery.

Once this first step is undertaken, and an environment of trust and transparency has been created, I move on to use music as therapy. I usually offer five daily sections per week of 30 minutes online using music, discussing and exploring songs and lyrics. These 30 minutes of music therapy can be 5 minutes listening for relaxation, five minutes listening to a couple of songs and the rest of the time discussing the lyrics and attempting to bridge the internal universe of the sufferer with the external reality. This is both complicated and simple, but basically it is to use particular the experiences of the sufferers and see if any songs and lyrics will help toward finding a possible solution for the experiences. It is also important to note that some songs can be disturbing to sufferers, so these must be eliminated from the list of helpful songs.

For example, I have used XXXTenctation's song, "Schizophrenia," with good results. The final message suggests to the listener not to give up and to struggle to overcome the voices and hallucinations.

> *I ain't seen the other side plentifully*
> *'Til the end I'll, 'til the end I'll fight*
> *There's another mind deep in me*

Don't know what's gotten into me
I ain't seen the other side plentifully
'Til the end I'll, 'til the end I'll fight
Don't give up, don't give up!
Don't give up, don't give up!
Don't give up, don't give up! (repeat)

If nothing else, this song gives some sufferers courage to try things towards recovery, which I suggest during the therapy. It is impossible for me here to describe methods in more detail, because knowledge of psychology and psychological methods is required so that offering music therapy to people with schizophrenia is not something that can be done by a non-trained person.

Songs of the Beach Boys are also very helpful, possibly because composer Brian Wilson suffers with schizoaffective disorder. Helping sufferers learn stories of successful people with schizophrenia, particularly artists, is also extremely helpful. As part of therapy, introducing sufferers to mental health experts who suffer with schizophrenia, such as a law professor like Elyn Saks[1], or well known English psychologist, Rufus May https://rufusmay.com/, who suffers with schizophrenia and has now recovered, is extremely important.

Above all, it is essential for people with schizophrenia to create a supportive network where art is the main activity of discussion. Music therapy promotes the practice of discussing and creating music with other people, so that socialization is a critical element of music therapy. Music promotes social activities and this is perhaps one of the most important benefits to sufferers. Recovering through music can be an extremely powerful and wonderful journey of self-healing and positive discoveries.

---

[1] www.ted.com/talks/elyn_saks_a_tale_of_mental_illness_from_the_inside
Also available at www.AlfredoZotti.org/music-therapy

7 | Anxiety, Depression and Music Therapy

While anxiety and depression are two different conditions, many people who suffer with anxiety also have depression and vice versa. There is a clear link between these two conditions, and also, most of the music that helps anxiety can also help depression. This is why I have combined the two disorders in one chapter. I will begin with anxiety and then move onto depression.

Anxiety is a very common mental health problem affecting a large percentage of the world's population. An estimated 275 million people around the world suffer with anxiety (Fleming, 2019). Given this, it is important to provide some in-depth information, starting with a close look at symptoms and interventions, to undestand such a common but debilitating problem.

Social phobia is one area of anxiety, and given that people in the music and entertainment industries, as well as famous people, experience it, I find it interesting and pertinent to look at it as an important example. After presenting information about social phobia, I will then move on to discuss how music therapy may be helpful.

This discussion defines social phobia and describes a variety of symptoms associated with this severe disorder, which can gravely affect a person's life and isolate them from society. Because depression often leads to social phobia and isolation, this section, while describing social phobia, is also pertinent for depression in that many symptoms overlap.

Social phobia is one of seven major anxiety disorders classified in the DSM-V (2013) as fear of social situations, where the person believes that he/she is exposed to the criticism and scrutiny of strangers. Its prevalence rate is between 10 and 16% of the population (Andrew et al., 2003; DSM-V-TR Page et al., 2013) and statistics of co-morbidity with depression are quite high compared to other anxiety disorders (Douglass, 2001; Heimberg et al., 1999). The main fear is that the sufferer will show their symptoms and behavior and consequently lose face in public (Clark, 2001). These intrusive thoughts are cognitive symptoms that give rise to anxiety, which in turn leads to more intrusive thoughts.

Another cognitive symptom is the desire to be loved and respected by everyone and others must appreciate that everything the sufferer does. However, this will not happen, because they will rely on past negative and anxious experiences and beliefs to relive these in present situations, creating a vicious circle that perpetuates the social phobia (Freeman et al., 1991). According to Page et al. (2011), there are two main groups of social phobia: specific or performance social phobia, such as fear of public speaking, and generalized social phobia, where the person experiences fear and anxiety in varied social situations. The establishment of a proper diagnosis of social phobia requires the presence of at least three symptoms for adults, and one for children, listed in the DSM-V TR. Attacks of social phobia are conceptualized in terms of how the individual responds to triggers, which differs from individual to individual.

The DSM-V outlines the following criterion to make a diagnosis of depression. The individual must be experiencing five or more symptoms during the same 2-week period and at least one of the symptoms should be either (1) depressed mood or (2) loss of interest or pleasure.

- Depressed mood most of the day, nearly every day.

- Markedly diminished interest or pleasure in all, or almost all, activities most of the day, nearly every day.

- Significant weight loss when not dieting or weight gain, or decrease or increase in appetite nearly every day.

- A slowing down of thought and a reduction of physical movement (observable by others, not merely subjective feelings of restlessness or being slowed down).

- Fatigue or loss of energy nearly every day.

- Feelings of worthlessness or excessive or inappropriate guilt nearly every day.

- Diminished ability to think or concentrate, or indecis-iveness, nearly every day.

- Recurrent thoughts of death, recurrent suicidal ideation without a specific plan, or a suicide attempt or a specific plan for committing suicide.

To receive a diagnosis of depression, these symptoms must cause the individual clinically significant distress or impairment in social, occupational, or other important areas of functioning. The symptoms must also not be a result of substance abuse or another medical condition.

Application of Music Therapy for Anxiety and Depression

What role does music therapy play in the aid of anxiety and depression, and what are my personal experiences while helping sufferers use music as a therapeutic tool? I will start by saying that most people experiencing severe depression do not usually like to listen to any music. It is as if that area of the brain that deals with music shuts off. This is because depression tends to cause people to lose their motivation. Those who can stand to listen to some music while depressed are a minority but these are the easiest to benefit from music while depressed.

Some experienced commentators rightly argue that sad music can have negative outcomes for people with depression. Studies have shown that sad music can aggravate depression, as this can fuel rumination, particularly if along with the sad music there are sad words. So, what should depressed people do? Not listen to music? Not listen to sad music? It all depends. We know that in periodic depression, anxiety and PTSD, episodes have to take their course, but it is usually the case, with some exceptions, that negative symptoms lift sooner or later. In some cases, sad music can speed up the course of the depression in the sense that the person has to go down further before they can get better. This has happened to me when listening to sad music. Sad lyrics have helped me get further down with my depression, and then I was able to get out of it. I feel that in some rare cases, sad songs and sad lyrics may provide evidence that other people go through profound struggles, and this helps in that we realize we are not alone with our suffering.

It is important now to state that each case must be treated as separate and unique, and while music therapy is evidence-based practice, it is impossible to adhere to anything strictly because people vary immensely. Each of us is a universe. Of course, this process can often be accompanied by great anxiety. When to do this is the issue, but usually a good music therapist with good, sound knowledge of psychology can assist the patient in going down further with their depression, therefore speeding up the process and safely reaching a point where the depression starts to lift.

Of course, the helper or therapist should keep in constant touch with the sufferer during the process. I have done this many times, even on my wife and myself. I found that getting more depressed, at times, would speed up the course of the depression and help me move towards recovery. However, it is important to be cautious, because listening to sad songs can lead to suicidal ideation. In this sense, unless there is a music therapist present to monitor things, it is advisable not to listen to sad songs while depressed.

In other instances, some sufferers may benefit from listening to positive and happy music, particularly coupled with happy and hopeful lyrics. In my journeys as a mental health helper for sufferers, I have not had the opportunity to help many people with depression. I have experience with many people with anxiety, mostly by using guided relaxation with music, such as the one I describe below, which is freely available online.

Case Study: Judy Wright

Judy Wright has been a friend for many years now. We never met in person, but have spent many hours communicating online and we were once writing on depressionconnection.org, a self-help website from Health Central in America. We both recognize the fact that music saved our lives and it continues to do so, and every day we are ever so grateful to be performing artists because playing music or singing can truly lift our spirit up at times when we feel down due to our depression. Here is Judy's story.

~ ~ ~

I think I've been depressed most of my life, but the first major episode I remember was when I was 12. I spent several months in bed with rheumatic fever — I could only leave to use the bathroom or to go to the doctor. After I was ambulatory again, I went through horrible insomnia until one night, I just broke down crying, thinking about stuff like my parents dying some day, etc. Actually, there was constant arguing and yelling in our house—my parents fought all the time, and my dad would scream at whoever was ticking him off at the time, so loudly the neighbors could hear it even when the windows were closed. For those three months, I had no life outside that room, other than to escape in books. But I always remember being afraid to feel joy or anything close to it, and I think the depression usually took the form of numbness. I would lie in bed and listen to the yelling.

Depression has wreaked havoc on my marriage at times, nearly cost me my job and isolated me from friends and family. Both of my adult sons have suffered from it since they were pre-teens, and the older one attempted suicide twice. I could say that this is a sign that it's genetic, and that may be partly true, but I'm sure my own depression had some influence on the mental health of my sons.

[Author's note: Judy is trying to express that both genetics and the environment are important. For a child to mimic a mental illness means that the child can develop a mental illness. So genetics may be a factor in transmission of depression through generation but for a child to mimic the parent's mental illness is also a problem in that it can also trigger a mental illness particularly if the genetic are predisposed to a trigger.]

My younger son is also on the autism spectrum and developmentally disabled, so that has posed an additional challenge when treating his depression. I know several people in my mother's family who were probably depressed, but undiagnosed as such. Even 40 years ago, there was so much stigma associated with any kind of mental illness, it was difficult to talk about and to admit to suffering from it.

My first experience with therapy began out of desperation, and I suffered much criticism from my family. My mother was certain that I spent each session bad-mouthing her, but I assured her that there were other things I had to talk about. My mother wasn't totally wrong, though. By the time I was 18, I was seriously depressed and probably had been for some time. I didn't know why, though. I didn't begin to know why for almost another 20 years, when memories started creeping in, and I realized that the little I remembered about my childhood was mostly sad and frightening.

I am the oldest of five children and there were four of us by the time I was five years old. We never had much money, and mostly what I remember is the constant yelling and screaming between my parents and at us kids. It didn't seem to matter what triggered it, especially for my dad. Something would just strike him the wrong way and he would start yelling obscenities and sometimes hit or kick us. Years later, my aunt told me that, on several occasions, he kicked me up and down a short flight of stairs in our house, and I remember him at one time kicking one of my brothers from the living room down the hallway and into his bedroom for something he had done.

What saved me, I think, from total despair were my maternal grandparents. I was able to spend a considerable amount of time with them, and even though my grandmother was fairly strict, she always managed to make me feel loved. I adored my grandfather, but he died when I was eight years old. Because my mother was so overwhelmed by his death, I was not allowed to grieve for him, and I still miss him to this day. On one occasion, I was permitted to see him in the hospital, shortly before he died from cancer. In those days, pain management was totally inadequate, and even I knew that he was suffering horribly. I can still remember the color of the suit he wore in his casket. But I could never cry. By then, I'd learned that crying brought punishment.

After my first son was born, I experienced post-partum depression without really understanding much about it. I felt strange not being at work, and my son was allergic to regular infant formula, then to soy milk, which caused him to be sick and cry a good share of the day. I'd cry when my husband left for work and cry when he came home. I ended up going back to work sooner than I'd planned, because I'd already spent four weeks waiting for my son to be born — he was a month overdue. Going back to work helped some, but I eventually went to the doctor and got put on an antidepressant, which I was able to discontinue after a few months. Four years later, after the birth of my second son, I got on medication much more quickly and averted a bad episode.

When my younger son was three years old, I began noticing that nothing felt right, and I was angry all the time, especially at my husband. I eventually got back into therapy but did not see a doctor for medication for a few more years after that. I hated myself and everyone else; there were times when I literally felt like I could have shot people at random if I had had a gun. I felt like I was looking for answers without knowing what the questions were. My therapist's reaction to my depression made me feel ashamed that I couldn't shake myself out of it. After five years of therapy, I was sick of getting nowhere and was beginning to get suspicious about why I couldn't remember most of my childhood and why even the word "childhood" felt like a heavy blanket over me. I decided to try hypnosis to see what I could uncover, and while I know that most people are wary of the reliability of memory retrieved in this manner, I was able to get a much bigger look at what my life had been like, much of it corroborated by a relative and by piecing together known facts. The memories were so real that I often experienced physical reactions to them, such as spontaneous bleeding.

I am still in the process of healing from the effects of abuse, still dealing with depressive episodes that are less severe than they used to be, but nevertheless, set me back every time. I found an online depression support group and discovered that maybe I could help others. Everyone who is depressed feels alone, even when he/she knows they're not. We deal with the stigma of it; it's usually not a fit topic for social discussion, yet it can eat up so much of our lives and poison our minds. So many members of this community have also experienced some kind of trauma, usually during childhood. The online site is a place where people can write about how they feel, ask questions, ask for support and discover that there are many others who have walked the same road before or are doing so right now. We help each other try to drown out the lies our depression is telling us.

It can be upsetting when you occasionally find someone writing in who is suicidal and appears unable to take in anything you say, but I've learned that there can be a point at which you have to let it go and trust in a higher power. We can support others, but the only ones we can 'save' are ourselves.

When I was a small child, from the time I was less than four years old, it was evidently quite easy for me to learn songs from the radio and from recordings. This is something I was told, and I don't have much memory of it, but I was often asked to "perform" at family gatherings. The times that I do remember seem rather devoid of feeling, probably because I survived my turbulent family life by shutting down. When I was four, my mother took me to a TV studio to audition for a children's amateur show, and I was chosen as one of the participants. I sang "The Song from Moulin Rouge," (Georges Auric, 1952) rather odd for a 4-year-old to sing, but I was told it would be "cuter" than singing the more-common "How Much Is That Doggie in the Window?" This was in the early 1950s, by the way, so a lot of people today would not have even heard of the latter song.

As the years went by, I enjoyed singing at school and in church and, when I was in high school, immensely enjoyed participating in the choir. It was an all-girls school, and we sang a lot of classical and sacred music. I would become so wrapped up in the music, and work so hard at it, that often times, right before a concert, I would totally lose my voice, which was extremely frustrating.

Looking back, I can see how singing has always been a means of both escape and emotional expression, which were badly needed when I was young. As an adult, I was able to participate in a couple of choirs for a few years, but then gave it up when employment and parenthood required most of my time.

Two years ago, I learned of a show choir that was looking for new members. Having been retired for a couple of years from an oppressive job situation, I was looking for some way to get back into music, so I auditioned and was accepted. For the first time, I am now also doing choreography and am finding it to be much more work than singing alone, but it's a good kind of work. Just going to practices and rehearsals can improve my mood if I'm having a bad day, because it requires me to interact with other people, which I tend to avoid if I'm feeling depressed. It's the music itself, though, that still allows me to transcend the day-to-day challenges that arise through living my life and having a family. Perhaps it's a form a mindfulness that makes it helpful, but it certainly does keep me focused on the present moment. If I can lose myself in it enough, it can invoke memories, both visual and emotional, that can color the present — almost like seeing things from a bigger perspective.

I don't know exactly how this works but singing does add another dimension to my life that feels unique to me in relation to my friends and family, who don't share that same interest (or passion, I should probably say). I value being able to pursue my love of music and hope I'm still able to sing for quite a few more years before my voice ages too much!

Anxiety and Guided Relaxation Therapy

Guided relaxation, as I have found through my effort of helping sufferers online, is the most effective way to help people to use music and words, combined in a way that helps the sufferers into deep relaxation. This is very helpful to both sufferers with anxiety and depression.

Slow Diaphragmatic Breathing

- Find a nice spot in one of your favorite rooms of your house and sit, possibly on a comfortable chair.

- Put some music on that you find relaxing.

- Put your hands on your belly.

- Start breathing slowly, calmly and deeply. Imagine that your upper torso is like a vase that you have to fill with air. Let the air go right down your belly, and imagine that the air can get past the belly right down below your navel. Continue to do this calmly as you relax further.

- Breathe in and out slowly, counting to 5 both when you inhale and when you exhale.

- Continue to breathe while slowing down the whole process as much as possible. Take your time, because the purpose here is to breathe slowly, and constantly taking your time in doing so and enjoying the breathing as you listen to music.

  Continue to practice each day for about 5 days, and then move onto the next stage, which is guided relaxation. This is because you first need to learn how to breathe with breathing exercises. One of the best guided relaxations that I found is "Healing Space: A spoken word guided meditation for deep relaxation" available at www.AlfredoZotti.org/music-therapy

For the guided relaxation, continue to do it one session each day for about one month. This should reduce your anxiety by far, and also improve your depressive moods. Breathing is central to anxiety, because anxiety is a disorder not only of your mind, but also of your breathing (Martin, 2013). Please remember that it is important not to do any kind of relaxation while driving or doing something that can potentially be dangerous, such as using machinery. It is important to just sit down and relax whenever doing any guided relaxation.

Finally, for both anxiety and depression, the secret is to find music that alleviates these symptoms and that works well just for you. For this purpose, it is important to engage in trial and error. See what helps and what doesn't, because, as I have stated, we are all different.

Mindfulness

Another thing that truly helps is mindfulness, which derives from principles of Buddhism. This is one application of the Buddhist practice of mindfulness that I have used with many people who find their work to be meaningless, boring or distressing. What I suggest is getting immersed in the job as if nothing else exists and it becomes self-rewarding.

After much experimentation and critical observation, I've found that when one is creating something that they are passionate about, as in a hobby or rewarding profession, one tends to forget everything and become involved in the work. I tend to forget my problems and my moods, and I get involved with the work. It is a wonderful experience to become lost in the work and to forget that one exists. I think all real artists experience this.

During my journey in the attempt to help people, I have also communicated with sufferers who have been mental health professionals at one stage of their lives. Here is what one such friend, who has bipolar I disorder writes:

> Mindfulness is a way to move past conditioned thoughts and the emotional reactions and behaviors that follow. By being non-judgmentally aware of a thought, there is no emotional or behavioral reaction to it. The thought can be observed. If emotionally disturbing, the thought can be faced and analyzed, instead of repressed with negative emotions attached and further conditioned in the mind. One can then choose the right way to act, based on a realistic view of the present moment without the reactions of past conditioning. Becoming aware of the body and mind are ways to sense emotional and bodily reactions to conditioned, irrational thoughts that automatically insert themselves in the conscious mind and irrational thoughts that are a common occurrence.

A parent can abandon a child for many reasons, sometimes irrational and selfish, sometimes out of love. They are the reasons of the parent and not the fault of the child. The child can grow bitter, blaming the parent for the suffering they feel, or they can blame themselves. In both cases, the suffering is created in the mind of the child. The abandonment is real. The suffering is created. Abandonment is not a reflection on the worth of the child. It is the action of the parent doing the best he/she can with what he/she has at the time.

The ego is the repository of past experiences, the situations, how we dealt with them, the results at the time and interpretations of the self-image in relation to these events. The ego is a tool we use to interact with the world around us based on these experiences.

Some of this information may once have seemed relevant to the irrational mind of a child, or at the time of the event, and most of it is irrational and cannot be applied to present events realistically as each event is unique.

My story is me, all the people ever in my life are me, all my possessions are me, all of my accomplishments are me, all the labels I attach to myself are me, all these things are me, describing myself by occurrences or things outside.

I am attached to all of them, without them I am empty, not myself, as I have built me out of them. If I am separated from them, I feel I have lost a part of me, they are a part of who I am. If I feel a lack of an attachment I feel I deserved, I am empty, as a part of myself is missing.

I have created my experiences and held them as treasures—good and bad. I have made myself out of others and things, and, along with them, experiences tell my stories of who I am, who I have created me to be.

I am not myself but a shroud I call myself, I created for myself in ways I choose and do not choose to perceive. I am living the past, never present, to fully appreciate the moment as I truly am. Who am I without my past, without the attachments to make me whole and set me apart from all others?

What is behind this created self? Have I created the other as others have, creating separation by this individual self an individual self-created through interpretation and judgment, inherently irrational and described by the role one plays or the possessions one has? This is the shroud of self we see the world through. How can one ever observe, be aware of the moment as it truly is, through this shroud?

Because in my effort to help people with mental illness, I have not had the opportunity to truly help people with depression, except for a handful of friends, my wife and myself. I asked my friend, Bob Rich, who has been a psychologist for about three decades, about helping those with depression. I explained to him that while I have helped lots of people with bipolar, Alzheimer's, autism and schizophrenia, I was not really confident about depression. As I have argued, people with depression tend to avoid any activity—particularly music.

8 Conclusion

There are many applications of music in psychotherapy. In this book, I have discussed some of the ways in which I combine music and psychology to help people. It is very important to emphasize that neither music nor psychotherapy are cures for any disability, mental or physical. What really matters is the special relationship between therapist and client, precisely as Carl Rogers with his theories on the person-centered approach (Davidson and Neale, 1990) had described many years ago.

In chapter two, I have discussed my attempt to help some people with Alzheimer's. One of my main points was that while music memories are not affected by the disease, these music memories can be stimulated and helped to take on non-musical memories, or at least to stimulate them. This idea was based on the notion that the brain is plastic. In addition, we have seen, from evidence based practice and research, how playing an instrument, but particularly the piano, can stimulate the whole brain and enhance memory areas in people with Alzheimer's. I discussed how the simple practice of using little songs to help sufferers achieve and remember everyday tasks is efficient and, above all, how music reduces anxiety, promotes wellbeing and gives sufferers a novel and more positive way to live their lives.

In chapter three, I defined mental illness, and in chapter four, discussed how music can be of assistance to people with bipolar disorder. Benefits of listening to songs, particularly lyrics that are chosen for specific purposes, moods and symptoms, are clearly discussed, particularly the vicarious element where the sufferer finds that the feelings and actions of a songwriter, through their songs, are similar to their experiences. I discussed how music could help sufferers to cope with the most distressing situation, as was the case for my wife. In this sense, music becomes a copying tool and a friend. Finally, I discussed how music can help sufferers by giving them an identity and a purpose, especially if they sing along to the songs and create a little song library for themselves. It is then that the lyrics can help sufferers create an identity for themselves, particularly when confused, depressed or anxious.

In chapter five, I discussed autism; specifically, the first lessons with students with autism, how it is important not to pressure them but to let them initiate the musical journey through discovery and self-participation. I demonstrated that I always let them begin by becoming curious of what was happening in the music room and how it is important to have an interesting room that can capture the attention of the autistic child. I discussed how the learning should be fun and not forced, or similar to work. The learning has to be fun. I argued that music can be a vehicle through which autistic children can engage in some social activities and build upon these in the future. We have seen from research how music can stimulate both sides of the brain and, in this sense, it encourages communication, social interaction and friendship. I discussed how girls are different from boys in that they are much better at hiding symptoms. This is possible because of gender differences and the way in which we conceptualize the female sex. The problem for therapist here is to be aware that girls can hide their autism well, and that because of cultural differences, their autism often goes unnoticed.

In chapter six, I discussed schizophrenia, particularly the fact that psychotic drugs do not always work and have terrible side effects. Music is good for sufferers, because it has a positive effect on the brain, promoting improvements in cognition and attention and leads to reduced symptoms of psychosis.

In chapter seven, I discussed anxiety and depression, because the two disorders, while different, share similarities and because many people who have anxiety also suffer with depression (and vice versa). Mindfulness and guided relaxation have proven invaluable, particularly to regulate breathing, heart rate and to generally promote wellbeing.

Music and psychology combined can be very powerful. However, it is important to remember that without establishing a good relationship between therapist and client, both music and psychology are useless.

From personal experience, I find that the special bond I create with the people I help is what really makes a difference. Most people have the ability to get out of the pit of despair in which they often find themselves. All they need is a helping hand and someone who has walked the walk and can show them the way out. I am fortunate that I suffer with bipolar II disorder, because all of my suffering and long road to recovery have made it possible for me to help others from direct experience, which not all therapists posses unless they have suffered directly with a mental disorder. Indeed, I do believe that the best therapists are those who have experienced a disability.

Seen from this perspective, both music and therapy are the perfect tools for the right therapist. A therapist has a natural gift, I believe, and that is great compassion for all people and the world, and high intelligence in all areas, not just rational intelligence but also spiritual and creative intelligence. There is no doubt in my mind that a therapist must have well-developed qualities that distinguish him/her as someone with the right personality for the job. These qualities are, among many, transparency with the client, honesty at all levels of communication, care and respect, patience, love and perseverance. Once the therapist has these qualities, combined with good knowledge of evidence-based practices and music, the therapist is ready to help.

References

ACE:

https://en.wikipedia.org/wiki/Adverse_Childhood_Experiences_Study

http://www.cdc.gov/violenceprevention/acestudy/index.html

Alvin J. (1966) *Music Therapy*. UK: John Baker Publishing.

American Psychiatric Association. (2013). *Diagnostic and statistical manual of mental disorders (5th ed.)*

Anderson, P., (2019). Music Cuts Need for Antipsychotics in Agitated Inpatients, *Medscape Online* retrieved from: www.medscape.com/viewarticle/913205

Andrews, G., Creamer, M., Crino, R., Hunt, C., Lampe, L., & Page, A. (2003). *The treatment of anxiety disorders: Clinician guides and patient manuals* (2nd ed.). New York, NY: Cambridge University Press.

Arky, B. Why Many Autistic Girls Are Overlooked, Child Mind Institute. Retrieved from https://childmind.org/article/autistic-girls-overlooked-undiagnosed-autism/ on March 2, 2020.

Bailey, C. H. & Kendel, E. R. (1993). Structural changes accompany memory storage. *Annual Review of Physiology. 55*, 397-426.

Balbag, M, A., Pedersen, N, L., and Gatz, M. (2014). Playing a Musical Instrument as a Protective Factor against Dementia and Cognitive Impairment: A Population-Based Twin Study. *International Journal of Alzheimer's Disease* Published online 2014 Dec. 2. Doi: 10.1155/2014/836748.

Barlow, D. H. (2002). *Anxiety and its disorders: the nature and treatment of anxiety and panic (2nd ed.)*. New York, NY: Guilford Press.

Beatty, M. J., Heisel. A. D., Hall, A. E., Levine, T.R. & La France, B, H. (2002). What can we learn from the study of twins about genetic and the environmental influences on interpersonal affiliations, aggressiveness and social anxiety?: a meta-analytic study. *Communication Monograph, 69*(1),1-18.

Becht M. C. & Vingerhoets A. J. J. M. (2002). Crying and mood change: a cross-cultural study. *Cogn. Emot. 16* 87–101 10.1080/02699930143000149

Beck, S. J. (2011). *Cognitive therapy: basic and beyond* (2nd.ed).New York, NY: The Guilford Press.

BeyondBlue.org.au. (2020). The science behind your smile. Retrieved October 04, 2020, from https://www.beyondblue.org.au/personal-best/pillar/in-focus/the-science-behind-your-smile

Bednarz, L. F. & Nikkel, B. (1992). The role of music therapy in the treatment of young adults diagnosed with mental illness and substance abuse. *Music Therapy Perspectives*, 10(1), 21-26. Doi: 10.1093/mtp/10/1/21

Bishop, N. A., Lu, T. & Yakner, B. A. (2010). Neural mechanisms of ageing and cognitive decline. *Nature* 464,529-535, doi: 10.1038/nature08983

Blackburn R. & Bradshaw T. (2014). Music therapy for service users with dementia: A critical review of the literature. J Psychiatric Ment Health Nurs. 2014;21(10):879–888.

Blacking, J. (1995). *How musical is man?*. Seattle: University of Washington Press.

Bruscia, K. E, (2014). *Defining music therapy* (3rd ed.) Barcelona Publishers.

Burton, L., Western, D. & Kowalski, R. (2012). *Psychology — 3rd Australian and New Zealand Edition.* (3rd ed.). Brisbane, Australia: John Wiley & Sons.

Carpenter, S. (2013). *Neuropsychoanalysis — Building Bridges Between Psychoanalysis, Neuroscience, Psychology and Psychiatry* [Electronic newsletter]. Retrieved from http://www.neuropsa.org.uk/what-freud-got-right

Castonguay, G. L., Boswell, F. J., Constantino, J. M., Goldfried, R. M. & Hill, E. C. (2010). Training implications of harmful effects of psychological treatments. *American Psychologist.* 65, 34-49.

Clark, D. M. & Wells, A. (1995). A cognitive model of social phobia. In R. G. Heimberg, M. R. Liebowitz, D. A. Hope & F.R. Schneider (Eds.), *Social Phobia* (pp. 69 -93). New York, NY: The Guildford Press.

Clarke, E., Dibben, N., & Pitts, S. (2012). *Music and mind in everyday life.* Oxford: Oxford University Press.

Coles, M. E., Hart, T. A. & Humberg, R. G. (2001). Cognitive behavioural group treatment for social phobia. In Crozier,W. R., & Alden, L. E. (Eds.), *International handbook of social anxiety: concepts, research and interventions relating to self and shyness* (pp. 449-470). London, UK: John Wiley and Sons Ltd.

Cooper, M. (2008). *Essential research findings in counselling and psychotherapy: the facts are friendly,* London: Sage.

Corey, G. (2011). *Theory and practice of counseling and psycho-therapy, student manual.* Wadsworth Publishing Co. Inc.

Cornelius R. R. (1997). Toward a new understanding of weeping and catharsis? in *The (Non) Expression of Emotions in Health and Disease* A. J. J. M. Vingerhoets & F. J. Published in: *Emotional expression and health.* Van Bussel (eds). https://pure.uvt.nl/ws/portalfiles/portal/582317/stougier.PDF

Corry, M. & Tubridy, A. (2001). *Going mad? Understanding mental illness.* Dublin: Newleaf, Gill & Macmillian Ltd.

Cross, I & Woodraft, G, E. (2009). Music as a communicative medium in R. Botha & C. Knight (Ed.). *The prehistory of language* (Vol. 1. Pp. 113-144). Oxford: Oxford University Press.

Darwin, C. (1998) *The expression of the emotions in man and animals* (3rd ed.). London: Harper and Collins Publishers.

De Sousa, A., & De Sousa J. (2010). Music Therapy in Chronic Schizophrenia. *Journal of Pakistan Psychiatric Society.* 7(1): 126—137.

Doidge, N. (2010). *The brain that changes itself.* (Rev. ed.). Victoria, Australia: Scribe Publications Pty Ltd.

Douglas S. (2001). Comorbid major depression and social phobia. *Primary Care Companion Journal of Clinical Psychiatry: Psychotherapy Casebook, 3*(4): 179-180.

Dubi, K., Rapee, R. M., Emerton, J. L. & Schneiring, C.A. (2008). Maternal modelling and the acquisition of fear and avoidance in toddlers: influence of stimulus preparedness and child temperament. *Journal of abnormal child psychology, 36,* 499 – 512.

Dweck, C. S. (2006), *Mindset: the new psychology of success.* New York: Random House.

Epstein, F, S., in Arky, B., (2020) Why Many Autistic Girls Are Overlooked. Child Mind Institute. Retrieved from https://childmind.org/article/autistic-girls-overlooked-undiagnosed-autism/ on the 4/2/ 2020.

Eustache, F., Lechevalier, B., Viader, F. & Lambert J. (1990). Identification and discrimination disorders in auditory perception: a report on two cases, *Neuropsychologia* 28: 282-91.

Finke, C., Esfahani, N. & Ploner, C. (2012). Preservation of musical memory in amnesic professional cellist, *Curr Biol* 22: R591-2.

Fleming, S. (2019), *This is the world's biggest mental health problem — and you might not have heard of it.* World Economic Forum. Retrieved from https://www.weforum.org/agenda/2019/01/this-is-the-worlds-biggest-mental-health-problem/ on the 3/20/2020.

Freeman, A., Pretzer, J., Fleming, B., & Simon, K. M. (1990). *Clinical application of cognitive therapy.* New York: Plenum Press.

Geretsegger, M., Elefant, C., Mössler, K., & Gold, C. (2014). *Music therapy for people with autism spectrum disorder.* The Cochrane library, (6). https://doi.org/10.1002/14651858.CD004381.pub3

Grieger, R. & Boyd, J. (1980). *Rational-emotive-therapy: a skills-based approach.* New York: Van Nostrand Reinhold.

Groussard, M., La Joie, R., Rauchs, G., Landeau, B., Chetelat, G. & Viader F. (2010). When Music and Long-Term Memory Interact. Effects of Musical Expertise on Functional and Structural Plasticity in the Hippocampus. *PLos ONE* 5(10):e13225. http://doi.org/10.1371/journal.phone.0013225.

Hanon, C. L. (1928). *The virtuoso pianist in Sixty exercises for the piano*. New York: G. Schirmer.

Halladay, A. K., Bishop, S., Constantino, J. N., Daniels, A. M., Koenig, K., et al.. (2015). Sex and gender differences in autism spectrum disorder: Summarizing evidence gaps and identifying emerging areas of priority. *Molecular Autism,* 6(1). doi:10.1186/s13229-015-0019-y

He, H., Yang, M., Duan, M., Chen, X., Lai, Y., Xia, Y., Shao, J., Biswal, B. B., Luo, C., & Yao, D. (2018). Music Intervention Leads to Increased Insular Connectivity and Improved Clinical Symptoms in Schizophrenia. *Frontiers in neuroscience,* 11, 744. https://doi.org/10.3389/fnins.2017.00744

Heimberg, R. G., Stein, M, B., Hiripi, E. & Kessler. R. C. (2000). Trends in the prevalence of social phobia in the United States: a synthetic cohort analysis of changes over four decades. *Eur Psychiatry*, 15, 29-37.

Holmes, J. (1993). *Between art and science: essay in psychotherapy and psychiatry*. New York: Routledge.

Hope, D. A., Burns, J. A., Hyes, S. A., Herbert, J. D. & Warner, M.D. (2010). Automatic thoughts and cognitive restructuring in cognitive behavioral group therapy for social anxiety disorder. *Cognitive Therapy Research*, 34, 1-12.

Insel, T. (2013). Director's blog: antipsychotics: taking the long view [Electronic mailing list message] Retrieved from http://www.nimh.nih.gov/about/director/2013/antipsychotics-taking-the-long-view.shtml

Ipser, J. C., Carey P., Dhansay, Y., Fakier, N., Seedat, S. & Stein D.J. (2006). Pharmacotherapy augmentation strategies in treatment-resistant anxiety disorders. *Cochrane Database Syst Rev*. Oct 18(4):CD005473.

Jamison, K. R. (2014). Bipolar disorder and the creative mind. CNN. http://www.cnn.com/2014/08/14/opinion/jamison-depression-creativity/

Johnson, J. K & Chow M. L. (2015). Hearing and music in dementia. *Handb Clin Neurol.* 129:667–687. [https://www.ncbi.nlm.nih.gov/pmc/articles/PMC4809670/

Kessler, R. C., Berglund, P., Demler, O., Walters, E. E. & Jin, R. (2005). Lifetime Prevalence and Age-of-Onset Distributions of DSM-IV Disorders in the National Comorbidity Survey Replication, *Archives of General Psychiatry* 62(6): 593-602.

Khalfa, S., Roy, M., Rainville, P., Della Bella, S. & Peretz I. (2008). Role of tempo entainment in psychophysiological differentiation of happy and sad music? *Int J Psychphysiol* 68:17-26

Koelsh, S. (2009). A neuroscientific perspective of music therapy *Annals of the New York Academy of Sci.* 1169:374-84. doi: 10.1111/j.1749-6632.2009.04592.x. https://www.ncbi.nlm.nih.gov/pubmed/19673812

Koelsch, S., & Jäncke, L. (2015). Music and the heart. *European Heart Journal,* 36(44), 3043-3049. doi:10.1093/eurheartj/ehv430

Lai, M.C., Lombardo, M.V., Ruigrok, A.N., Chakrabarti, B., Wheelwright, S.J. & Auyeung, B. (2012). Cognition in males and females with autism: similarities and differences. *PLoS One.* 7:e47198. doi: 10.1371/journal.pone.0047198https://www.ncbi.nlm.nih.gov/pmc/articles/PMC3474800/

Legg J. T., (2018). *Everything you need to know about autism.* Retrieved from https://www.healthline.com/health/autism

Lutz,W., Sanderson,W., & Sherbow, S. (2008). The coming acceleration of global population ageing. *Nature,* 451, 716-719. Doi: 10.1038/nature06516.

Martin, G. & Pear, J. (2020). *Behaviour modification: what it is and how it works.* Pearson Educational International.

Martin, P. (2013). *Depression and Anxiety in Preschoolers.* Author manuscript; available in PMC 2013 Oct 22. Published in final edited form as: Depress Anxiety. 2013 Apr; 30(4): 315–320. Published online 2013 Mar 6. doi: 10.1002/da.22076

Maté, G. (2010). *In the Realm of Hungry Ghosts: Close Encounters with Addiction.* Berkley, California :North Atlantics Books.

McChesney-Atkins, S., Davies, K.G., Montouris, G.D., Silver, J.T. & Menkes, D.L. (2003). Amusia after right frontal resectionfor epilepsy with singing seizures: case report and review of the literature, *Epilepsy Behav* 4: 343-347.

Naukkarinen, H. (1984). Music Therapy in Schizophrenia. In: Houldin V. (Ed). *Social Psychiatry,* 231-236. doi:10.1007/978-1-4684-4535-0_24

Neenan, M. & Dyden, W. (2011). *Rational emotive behavioural therapy in a nutshell.* (2nd ed.). London: Sage Publications.

Nilsson, U. (2009). Soothing music can increase oxytocin levels during bed rest after open-heart surgery: A randomised control trial. *Journal of Clinical Nursing,* 18(15), 2153-2161. doi:10.1111/j.1365-2702.2008.02718.x

Nyklíček, I., & Vingerhoets, A. (2002). *(Non-)Expression of emotions in health and disease.* Abingdon: Brunner-Routledge.

Niznikiewicz, M. A., Spencer, K. M., Dickey, C., Voglmaier, M., Seidman, L. J., Shenton, M. E. & McCarley R.W. (2009). Abnormal pitch mismatch negativity in individuals with Schizophrenia.. 110(1-3):188-93. doi: 10.1016/j.schres.2008.10.017. *Epub 2009 Mar 27.schizotypal personality disorder.*

Page, A. C., Menzies, R. G., Bryant, R. A. & Abbott, M. (2011). Anxiety disorders (pp. 45-90). In E. Rieger (Ed.), *Abnormal psychology: Leading researcher perspectives.* (2nd ed). Melbourne: McGraw-Hill.

Pearson, C., Mann, S., & Zotti, A. (2017). *Art therapy and the creative process: A practical approach.* Ann Arbor, MI: Loving Healing Press.

Peters, J. S. (2000). *Music therapy: An introduction.* Springfield, IL: Charles C. Thomas Publishers, Ltd.

Porter, R. S., Kaplan, J. L., Lynn, R. B., & Reddy, M. T. (2018). *The Merck manual of diagnosis and therapy.*

Pull, C. B. (2005). Current status of virtual reality exposure therapy in anxiety disorder. Editorial review. *Current Opinion in Psychiatry*, 18, 7-14.

Rea, C., MacDonald, P. & Carnes, G. (2010). Listening to classical, pop, and metal music: An investigation of mood. *Emporia State Research Studies.* Vol. 46, no. 1, p. 1-3. http://academic.emporia.edu/esrs/vol46/rea.pdf

Read, J., van Os, J., Morrison, A. P., & Ross, C. A. (2005). Childhood trauma, psychosis and schizophrenia: a literature review with theoretical and clinical implications. *Acta Psychiatr Scand*, 112: 330–350.
doi: 10.1111/j.1600-0447.2005.00634.x

Rich, R. (2019). *From depression to contentment: A self-therapy guide*. Ann Arbor, MI: Loving Healing Press.

Rieger, E. (2011). *Abnormal psychology: Leading researcher perspectives.* (2nd ed.). Melbourne, Australia: McGraw-Hill.

Rogers, C. (1951). *Client-centered therapy: Its current practice, implications and theory.* London: Constable ISBN 978-1-84119-840-8.

Rogers, C. (1957). The necessary and sufficient conditions for therapeutic personality change. *Journal of consulting psychology, 21(2),* 95-103.

Salisbury, D. F., Shenton, M. E., Griggs, C. B., Bonner-Jackson, A. & McCarley, R.W. (2002). Mismatch negativity in chronic schizophrenia and first-episode schizophrenia. *Arch Gen Psychiatry.* 59(8):686-94 doi: 10.1001/archopsyc.59.8.686.

Samson, S. & Peretz, I. (2005). Effects of prior exposure on music liking and recognition in patients with temporal lobe lesions. *Ann N Y Acad Sci* 1060: 419-28.

Schellenberg, E. G., Corrigal, K.A., Dys, S.P. & Malti, T. (2015). *Group music training and children's prosocial skills. PLoS ONE.* 10:e0141449. doi:10.1371/journal.pone.0141449.

Sharda, M., Tuerk, C., Chowdhury, R., Jamey, K., Foster, N., Custo-Blanch, M., Tan, M., Nading, A., Hyde, K. (2018). *Music improves social communication and auditory-motor connectivity in children with autism, Translational Psychiatry*, Published online 8: 231. Doi: 10.1038/s41398-018

Simonelli, D. (2013). *Working class heroes: Rock music and british society in the 1960s and 1970s*, Lanham, MD: Lexington Books.

Sismey, G. & Gillett, G., (2015). *Music Therapy as a treatment for Schizophrenia,* retrieved from https://www.cebm.net/wp-content/uploads/2015/10/Music-therapy-as-a-treatment-for-schizophrenia-GS-and-GG.pdf

Smith, M., Segal, J., & Hutman, T. *Helping Your Child With Autism. HelpGuide. Your trusted guide to mental health and wellbeing* http://www.helpguide.org/articles/autism-learning-disabilities/helping-your-child-with-autism-thrive.htm

Stein, M. B. & Stein, D. J. (2008). Social anxiety disorder. *Lancet. 29*, 1115-25.

Stoner, G. Fung, R., Gil-da-Costa and Albright, T. (2013). Salk researchers develop new model to study schizophrenia and other neurological conditions: model should have widespread application for pharmaceutical research. Retrieved from http://www.salk.edu/news/pressrelease_details.php?press_id=636

Taylor, S., Woody, S., Koch, W. J., McLean, P., Paterson, R. J. & Anderson, K. W. (1997). Cognitive restructuring in the treatment of social phobia. *Behavior Modification, 21,* 487–511.

Taylor, S. E., Klein, L. C., Lewis, B. P., Gruenewald, T. L., Gurung, R. A. & Updgegraph, J. A. (2000). Biobehavioural responses to stress in females: tend and befriend, not fight or flight. *Psychological review, 107,* 411- 429.

Todd. G. , Michie, P.T., Schall, U., Ward, P.B., Catts, V.S. (2011). Mismatch negativity (MMN) reduction in schizophrenia — Impaired prediction — error generation, estimation or salience? *Int. J. Psychophysiol.* (2011), doi:10.1016/j.ijpsycho.2011.10.003.

Tuggart, A. (2011). *A critique of CBT- part 1*. Retrieved from http://andrewjtaggart.com/2011/10/26/a-critique-of-cbt-part-1/ on April 2, 2013.

Västfjäll, D. (2001). Emotion induction through music: A review of the musical mood induction procedure. *Musicae Scientiae, 5*(1_suppl), 173-211. doi:10.1177/10298649020050s107

Vocabulary.com   https://www.vocabulary.com/dictionary/prosody retrieved on 3/10/2020

Walkup, J.T., Albano, A. M., Piacentini, J, Birmaher, B., Compton, S.N. & Sherrill, J.T. (2008). Cognitive behavioral therapy, sertraline, or a combination in childhood anxiety. *N Engl J Med*.

Watt, M. C. & Di Francescantonioa, S. (2010). *Childhood Learning Experiences in the Development and Maintenance of Anxiety Disorders*. Retrieved from: http://www.anxietybc.com/learning-and-anxiety

Werling, D. M. & Geschwind, D. H. (2013). Understanding sex bias in autism spectrum disorder. *Proc Natl Acad Sci USA*. 110:4868–9. doi: 10.1073/pnas.1301602110. https://www.ncbi.nlm.nih.gov/pmc/articles/PMC3612630/

Zotti, A. (2014). *Alfredo's journey: An artist's creative life with bipolar disorder*. Ann Arbor, MI: Modern History Press

Zotti, A. (2018). *Got bipolar?: An insider's guide to managing life effectively*. Ann Arbor, MI: Loving Healing Press.

About the Author

Alfredo Zotti is the son of the late Luciano Zotti (https://it.wikipedia.org/wiki/Luciano_Zotti), Italian composer, orchestra conductor and musical director, and his wife, Cristina Zotti.

In 1974, Alfredo, his parents and brother, Giovanni, migrated to Sydney, Australia. At first, life was difficult, because the family worked in a wood factory for little pay. As time went on, Luciano began to work as a musician and music teacher and life slowly improved for him and his family.

In 1981, after many traumatic events, Alfredo began his lifelong challenge of living with bipolar disorder. He quickly hit rock bottom, spending time as a homeless person and turning to street drugs and alcohol to medicate his symptoms. But life improved after hospitalization and careful outpatient monitoring.

Alfredo married Cheryl MacDonald, who also suffers with bipolar disorder, and he was able to enroll in a university course. He gained an honours degree in sociology and anthropology. He went on to study clinical psychology at the University of Newcastle, but he did not complete his degree, because he felt that academia had taken the wrong path in the prevention and cure of mental illnesses. He completed some courses at first, second and third year level, with distinction and high distinction. Alfredo also studied piano and was able to attain the grade 8 skill in piano.

Today, Alfredo is the full-time caregiver for his wife, who suffers from a number of disabilities. He also regularly raises funds for his local hospital, Gosford Hospital, by organizing fundraiser nights, where he plays with other musicians. So far, he has helped to raise thousands of dollars. The money goes toward the needs of the hospital's patients with mental disorders. Alfredo also writes an online journal, *The Anti Stigma Crusaders*, which he uploads regularly at two or three month intervals.

Additionally, Alfredo provides support for online sufferers and uses his art to help people. While he is not a qualified music therapist, he does use music and art to help people online. Some mental health professionals often consult him for his lived experience and knowledge of psychology and music. He has written three books, including this one, two published and one that is free online. He also contributes by giving talks at universities about his experience with bipolar disorder. Learn more at www.AlfredoZotti.org.

Index

More than a just a journey, Alfredo gives us a blueprint for humane treatment of mental illness.

In 1981, twenty-three year-old Alfredo Zotti began his lifelong challenge of living with bipolar II disorder. He quickly hit rock bottom, spending time as a homeless person and turning to street drugs and alcohol to medicate his symptoms. After hospitalization and careful outpatient monitoring, he became a successful musician and completed university. In 2004, he started to mentor sufferers of mental illness, and together, they developed an online journal. Alfredo now sees mental illness from a new perspective, not of disadvantages but advantages. In his words, "Having a mental illness can be a blessing if we work on ourselves."

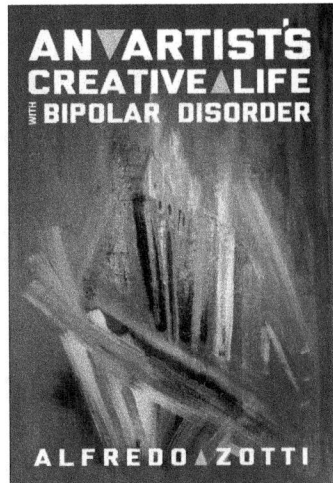

In this memoir and critique of mental illness, the reader will learn:

- How empathic listening and being with someone can help calm that person's symptoms
- The power of singing to create a safe space in a community
- Why spirituality can be a key component in the healing process
- The connections among mental illness, artistic expression and people who think differently
- The impact of childhood trauma on our psyche and its role in mental illness
- The dangers of antipsychotics and antidepressants
- The amazing connection between heart and brain and how we can cultivate it
- The challenges of love and marriage between partners with bipolar disorder

ISBN 978-1-61599-224-9

From Modern History Press

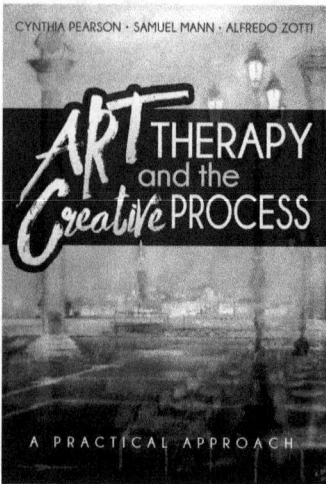

CYNTHIA PEARSON · SAMUEL MANN · ALFREDO ZOTTI

Art THERAPY and the Creative PROCESS

A PRACTICAL APPROACH

International voices from across the globe come together in *Art Therapy and the Creative Process* to share their perspectives on art, the artist's process and how art has been therapeutic for them.

In the first section, the three primary contributors—Alfredo Zotti, Samuel Mann and Cynthia Pearson—create a triple commentary on a piece of art. Zotti paints a picture, Mann analyzes it and Pearson writes a poem to complement it. In later sections, various artists share why they write, paint, play music or take photographs, including what their individual mediums mean to them, what they may mean to others, why they have chosen various art forms, how art allows them an opportunity to escape from the world and how it can also help them heal.

Artists will find kindred spirits in these pages. Lovers of literature, music and art—in all its forms—will gain insight into artists' souls, how they view the world a little differently and why. *Art Therapy and the Creative Process* gives art a purpose beyond what most of us usually think of it having—that art is a way to keep us all sane in a maddening world, and it gives us the opportunity to create something to heal the same world that wounds us.

"This book is a beautiful piece of work, and all concerned should be very proud. The human dimension, enhanced through art and expressive approaches, should be a much stronger part of mental health care."

— Professor Patrick McGorry, AO MD PhD, executive director, OYH Research Centre, University of Melbourne

ISBN 978-1-61599-296-6

From Loving Healing Press